The Unfinished

Books I-VI

The Unfinished

Books I-VI

Mark DuCharme

BLAZEVOX[BOOKS]
Buffalo, New York

The Unfinished: Books I-VI
By Mark DuCharme
Copyright © 2013 by Mark DuCharme

Published by BlazeVOX [books]

All rights reserved. No part of this book may be reproduced without the author's written permission, except for brief quotations in reviews.

Printed in the United States of America

Interior design and typesetting by Geoffrey Gatza

Cover photo by Rose DuCharme

First Edition
ISBN: 978-1-60964-140-5
Library of Congress Control Number: 2013942427

BlazeVOX [books]
131 Euclid Ave
Kenmore, NY 14217

Editor@blazevox.org

publisher of weird little books

BlazeVOX [books]

blazevox.org

21 20 19 18 17 16 15 14 13 12 01 02 03 04 05 06 07 08 09 10

BlazeVOX

Also by Mark DuCharme

Life Could Be A Dream (last generation press, 1990).
Emphasis (:that:, 1993).
i, a series (Burning Press, 1995).
4 sections from Infringement (Oasis Press, 1996).
Contracting Scale (Standing Stones Press, 1996).
Infringement. (*Light and Dust*, 1998).*
Three Works (Invasive Map). (Oasis Press, 1998).
Desire Series. (Dead Metaphor Press, 1999).
Near To. (Poetry New York/Meeting Eyes Bindery, 1999).
Anon [with Anselm Hollo, Laura E. Wright and Patrick Pritchett, with illustrations by
        Jane Dalrymple-Hollo]. (Potato Clock Editions, 2001).
Cosmopolitan Tremble. (Pavement Saw Press, 2002).
Infinity Subsections. (Meeting Eyes Bindery, 2004).
The Crowd Poems. (Potato Clock Editions, 2007).
The Sensory Cabinet. (BlazeVOX Books, 2007).
The Found Titles Project. (*Ahadadabooks.com*, 2009).*
Answer. (BlazeVOX Books, 2011).

*Electronic publication.

Acknowledgments

Parts of this work have appeared, at times in slightly different versions, in the following journals:

Blue & Yellow Dog: "There is a crack in my windshield," "To drive through night like smoke," "It rains a little in the repugnant mirror," and "As if to merge, by chromatic difficulties."

Colorado Review: "Like thinking under your skin" and "If you plunged my heart into a river."

Eleven Eleven: "To invert the mechanisms of untrapped sleep" and "Above/ The fields."

E•ratio: "Whenever I read a writer," "What, in utter/ Desecration lays," "The muted particulars are also free" and "To hear it alternately where it does not run."

Letterbox: "There are still no more of us," "The horizon does not make," and "Becoming the visible/ Gift."

New American Writing: "But naming can also mean vanishing," footnotes 11-15 and "To begin again with a mouthful."

On Barcelona: "To sing to ourselves while the dead inform us," footnotes 23-24, "Write a composition on the forms that silence takes," "The poem is another way of vanishing," "Is it, in the minutes we don't/ Pass."

Or: "I dreamed extending variables that this was all one work," "To get outside that sound," "endless as in night repeats," "We can collapse mazes….," "Here is the Book with its/ Excesses," "How can I make it disappear— this burden of naming," "It's night & you are not asleep," "Poetry, as I have said, is information," "Even if seeming to not sit still," "How much of this is made," "But to still come here in the unanswered questions" and "Is it we who are the trafficked?"

Otoliths: "The institution was coming," "Today is porous with material" and "The marvel at the side of a reference."

Pinstripe Fedora: "That I ate all the circles," footnotes 1-4, "What is it where we are starting," "Remember when the lights went out" and "Kisses as givens."

Poets for Living Waters: "To still be held, against an atrocity."

Raft: "To have no vocabulary for this hunger," "Logos as transitive," "When I say it will not bloom, it will not," "When I say it will not bloom, I mean to" and "At the double edge of being & saying."

Reconfigurations: "The ghost buildings" and "The scar is what we imagine."

Word For/Word: "Without seeming to provide other examples" and "We could extract this language in a cup."

"The birth and development of thought are subject to laws of their own, and sometimes demand forms of expression which are quite different from the patterns of logical speculation. In my view poetic reasoning is closer to the laws by which thought develops, and thus to life itself, than is the logic of traditional drama."
—Andrei Tarkovsky

"If reality is simply that
    which is accessible to reason
    when it folds over and
    it sticks up
Then sexuality is very optimistic—"
—Lyn Hejinian

"I love poetry because it's naturally incomplete."
—Eileen Myles

"Of anything that is, there
    might be more"
—Lyn Hejinian

"I thank you that the limit has finally been transgressed. That the hour has been shattered. But what do the splinters reflect?"
—Max Von Sydow's character, in
Ingmar Bergman's *Hour of the Wolf*

Table of Contents

The Unfinished

Books I-VI

BOOK I.

For the ghost

The Unfinished

To save or savor compromising reflections

In the heat only one of us would go

I'm tired of poetry, its gaps & spillage

The flavor of the night is not genuine

Night— its searing box of tunes

Lead me from it as if to shower

Someone I know with flavor— which leads from the scene

Like a box of knowledge interspersed with dew

If you believe me, which I doubt, you grand

Ventriloquist, you upstart

Of wild tenderness, you lunatic repairperson

Perhaps you will favor me with a song or two before I go

Some link to the rebellions of past stockrooms

The incommodious clash of crowds' brocades

Until someone else waits for me, whose hindsight is private

& I rend you this batch of chalk & bone

So uniquely out of tune with clouds' character

Composing & composed by vast idioms of joy

At clouds' domains— the very piracy which renders thinking out of tune

The Unfinished

Kisses as givens. The procedure
Was blasted by ecstatic trains
Or, curving into you
The signal of a reversal. Something
You say has driven me to sway
To turn up the outcome or stakes
Of a tasting
Your tongue at the least suspended
Air or rendez vous— an imbroglio foliage
Tasted or involuntary
On the brink of an ecstatic letdown

•

To consider the imaginary
While you wrap your long-stemmed glassware

In the park as if thinking were
Over

The parlances a heap of
Subject-
Positions in the positioning of an awry space

It's becoming a lacuna
For worn out birds
Again, before you say anything

Anything more in the admissions pliancy

Of having forgotten to speak

Or read your energy in the laughing vibrato

Of sad trees that you listen to

When we are aflame with unpacking apartments

To find the root note a lover's soot

A deciduous verticality like the poor man's appliance

A moot type   reversal of taxis

The Unfinished

Being seeing as glistening   what was
Risible in the park after intake
Becomes rinsed in finely
As a blanket of what now is sated

To say anything intricate
Or embossed
After splay of fissures
Breath of sudden rooms   the complete

Incorruptible as neon reverie—
The sadness in the park
Of not-summer:

All could shrivel   drop off bower

Poetry will be left

I dreamed extending variables that this was all one work, that clearly the patchwork circumstance of meeting or stopping lent some kind of jiffy brightness to the fact that writing *occurs* in days, which are themselves far from complete. Then do I question the bastard notion of completeness? I question the scope of the totality of writing which can be readily imagined. Letting the scales come off their notes; letting the notes themselves dig deeper into the particulate matter of words, words which *burst the matter open*. Writing is not thinking & it is not music, yet it bears a semblance to their bastard offspring. Studying will get you no further— yet without knowledge you are lost. Writing creates a frame. It is the sum of what is lost in spoken company. The written intrudes on quotidian outcomes, bypassing social strictures ~~structure~~ with its own necessity. The page, in other words, does stare, & when you stare back you are creating a conversation— a rupture in the easy consumption of the thicket of meaning(s). An indigestion, if you will. Troubling the understood.

after Spicer

The Unfinished

The sonnet is not dead, but I am hungry

I am here, thinking of words

Like dead doctor detective English

Thankful for the key to open doors

It is not night, you are awake

& I am telling so that shadows form upon the page

The belly, & apples singing mildly

In the comparison between trees & thighs

Night & what is seeming to tear open

Shot through with a catalogue of dreams

The vocabularies form an impression of me, though I am stable

In libraries vaster than orange night sky

Apollinaire is dead. Ted Berrigan died

We feed off dreams like hungry ghosts

The Unfinished

The offer of lunch must be taken with bravado
Until we finish being serious all the time
I'm finished. The room is frozen solid. We
Are an invention I mistake for breath

There is room between the planets to encompass us
The infinite incursions which your lips sustain
Biting character worn like a smile
Characters wearing legends which boys consume

To fully consume you, I must leave
To fully call you, I must listen to silence
To fully hear your voice, I must feel my pulse beat
To fully sing you to sleep, I must transcribe bird cries

To fully open myself to you I must feel
Your touch, even when sitting here alone

[1] Clean up the damp trees! Hunger is affected. In proportion to what we say is lost. Mangled, in case of the popular.

[2] It's the frivolity of calamity that really gets me off. The world explodes with the singing of bees. Does one "manhandle" a crisis, in tune with the exemptions of ringleaders? I think that waiting is not stopped. The cat rattles my pen.

[3] I cannot know the ulterior desires of fatalists until thrushes rush into disparate bodies. What seems sure is eased by moments of bribery, touching down on what is not quite said. Was there an instant where brainstorms eased troubled suction? Hell as a means of social delivery— the leveling of desire. Or else some wind which charts our need to fire up the local.

[4] Dispersed by intimate bluejays. In a hospital composed of language. To fuck in the meantime— though shadows are impaled by light. In the obscenity of a white page whose neatness troubles dreaming.

The Unfinished

Is all this chatter just for pay

Have we been meaning to hear from them

Without going to sleep? A song divides

       Us from the stockpile

What relief to dream in airtight cities

What meanings divide us now?

A question presupposes an answer

Triggers of the world at large

This is all very routinely on display

When I say that I'm sick of

       This work, what

Am I driving at? Or am

I driving when I say I am?   Aim

       For the place of dead records

Accept no deliveries

       From unwanted husbands. Turn up the airtight

Tinkering. Smile & look away

Compose an answer to which there are no

Questions. Get up & stumble—

       A sudden environment

Against which questions appear

The Unfinished

That I ate all the circles
Of freeways tilted
On dark circum-
ferences jostling

Eros sighed. There was a matador
Involved
A kind of sickly entertainment
When the moon runs away

The throes were wrestled from the landscape
At the limit of what strayed
Like the cries of passing children
Or pedestrians at midnight

At the limit of repeating
Where you do not sing
In order to frighten birds away
Tender as an overreaction

A lens toward which you do not smoke
Is spoken of publicly like the demoted
In the emotive publicity stills where angels play
With those who imagine them to be angels

Rain in boxes   the earth a lure
Edges of the night soaked humming

The Unfinished

What is, but nearly goes away

At the downside of a suggestion

Muted outside broken communities

In the terrorism of a reaction

Not to feel, but dream

Staged against the plastic

Rampant boxes which rail against storage

Imperfect with permission

Were I a box

An errant steerage

Would you go away

To the land of houses & subjects

You are talking to the books

To make a case for houses & subjects

In their arms, bursting with errancy

To gather positions for the cities you won't build

To be as profligate as a dumbwaiter

Before the invention of glass

Is to be someone who refuses to speak

But to children, in the language of unkempt yards

The Unfinished

That I listen, or can feel such rushing

Even when birds speak

Of the unconventionality of limbs

That the winds brush silent surfaces when we

Talk   when we talk we talk of cities

The commonality of surfaces in the afternoon

Over here where the bombs whisper

In silence

Which only breeds more silence

There is some form of thinking before bombs can drop

I want to know as physical event

Physicality which bursts like cities

& The amazements of grief

Until bombs are nearly sated, brushing against trees

The Unfinished

To get outside that sound

Or run into it later

Apparitionally until correct

With parakeets & the unthinking

From which we are exhumed, or overreacting

As a text is written on a flask

To spill into crowds while buttoned down

Coming at me *fully forced*

•

That the original flares up, or out of

When I'm thinking or behind myself

In a body of unreadiness

Readiness is often die-cut

This is an example of proficient vintners

A stain, or not to burn ~~while formed~~

With some of the tunes unwritten

•

Tom Waits would say this is too inverted

Under ramparts of blue day burning

Burning like ice in the railyard

I am often projected in purely suspect ways

I steal your vocabulary, though the moon is strangled

Beneath the prism of an overreaction

To inquisitors pricking

•

I feel differently in the air we breathe

I breathe you in the intensity of air itself

I knock over piles

Of books accidentally this is

Nothing new

Newness is overrated

The air surrounds you like my body

I dream we speak a different language

Which is everything that death abandons

[5] Listen to the way the intimate rush drowns out tropes & questions. I had almost forgotten that I needed sleep. Then the window broke & I ejaculated onto the content. It had been summer, the glare of longer days lending an optimistic hue to the proceedings. Rain doesn't fall on certain ventures. I remember the moon landing in your heart. I have an empirical sense of noon when you aren't here. Questioned to evade what looks, as a pen is stuck into the heart of dysphoria. Your name, a singsong development now the earth turns cold. Are there trees as bare as this?

[6] The exorbitant is outside song. I could offset the reflections of clouds on skyscrapers if thinking were more elephantine. As it is, the strangeness of language unmasks clock faces. At the stroke of twelve, when all singing bursts—

[7] Nothing is permeable on the face of twilight. Where skin is permeable meaning. Buildings photographically dissolved at sunset. To answer any question with a question. At the instability of retrieval, where words are clinging to your lips. Faces & evidence. You can make it new or make it up or make it ancient & strange or make it unimaginable to itself. As onlookers' lips purse with the ungainly.

The Unfinished

The institution was coming

Through the grammar of the institution the in-

stitution sways

Engendering an unrest like seminoles

Or any seminal confines

Whereas to have begun inclemently

Constructing particles which are beginning

To concur

At which what's risked is deafening combines

Confines of a proposed sleep

Darkening a piracy of intuition's subjects

It escapes through taking in the nakedly

Who, incomplete, are surfacing

As what's still visible in the

Dark

Where you are you   are

Destined toward whereof I speak

To reconnect its sway

Where? among the ghosts, still

Incomplete as night's dark language

Though sensible as incomplete parking

To thump the romantic party lurkers

Rioting in the eaves

While I collaborate with my   self

& With it stirs

Until what veers must cease

　2/

What does it mean to finish

What was said

Finish others' sentences

As if one were a Finn or an onlooker

Unwanting through repeat   delirium

Or rumor: I repeat

There is dust on the windowsills that no one looks

At   a steady mark of reflection

Whose "finishing touches" defy the outbound

The reckless, militantly inward

　3/

The poodle was rushed to the saloon
Adjacent as whispering   to what?
What was thought
　Written in *People*
I was a thing, an in-
　　complete statement
Shattered like pavement; it
　Was surfaces something
Complicated in   telling
　Closer than reflection— which starts
　　To complicate desire

　　　　　nearer than what

　　contains as surveys

that in night would still not mend

up to its suction or legend

outtake

surfaces a blank at even

4/

The woman

Called out *Hello*

But appeared

To be talk

ing to no

one

5/

Vast transit reap survey

The same if only   louder

Above surfaces (or surveys)

The chair was not

Or was it jerking

I couldn't have staged the

REPEAT   repeat sentences arisen

What's arrogantly concealed, above our

Tongues   shadows forge

Contorted as retorts

As if a gunbarrel, a loose sign

    To direct in trafficked dancing

Dare I repeat the idiom of an onrush

This imposition or air is sweeter than music

       Unerotic surcharge

     Autodenial

  6/

Four score and seven years agog

For scare and heaven's ears

Fair scare at heathens

Fear sere at _____

For scorned

F***

   We whose truths are outright gardens

      Score here at evidence

     Maybe heaven repeats

    An outright primate

   Agog, to scramble

  Until botched, like heaven's scare

7/

To still dream, at night repeating—
  & Bend like wings on

      impact

8/

endless as in night repeats. Still with shadows vanishing. To have forged a burnt-out world. Readers, whom I don't suspect. But underscore, in a kind of frantic retreat (wanderers wandered in rococo studies). Dusk mentioned again. The tune was settled up to the conventions of stopping or starting. Who grow impatient with the simple sampling as they are themselves the whiffs of driven artifacts. Nothing is finished which declares itself in debt to the history of these distractions. I thought not, remaining sticky as these points of an intersection surging. Poetry occurs at any moment. The world is a descriptive urge. At the beginning of our roadtrip, it was feared things would go a long way off. But the map is durable, & new projects wider any hint of anticipatory malice. The Good Captor berated the hirelings for their poor networking skills. But I continue to find legendary disturbances in all that furtively hints of evening. Like dusk on the tongue when it was important to sail. The bombshelters were strewn with relics. Hints of easy money which were quickly disfigured. Renouncing the figurative, as a shovel could be a document of the deforestation of the imagined. I had said "maybe," probably, in a flurry of exchangeable sketching. Decimated as a litany might be, in this context. I'm picturing the Big Picture now, but it's futile. Daylight throttles my perceptions & I become iffy as a nomadic bee. Or something less outright, a rhizomic declaration of common toil. The speculative paper had become brittle. It suspends an ending in the duration of its parlances, foiled as they are by ghosts of all that writing intends. "Writing intends capture," the Bad Captor observed, but her intent grew cloudy. It is, in the final estimate, a glint of lightning, a knob in the throat. Or all that writing cares to dream, endless, endless as this threshing of the syllables of bees, endless as in broken communion, endlessly submerged & merging, palpable as the horizon line at which no one cares to stand— or those determinations of no one blurred, shattered in an outline—

after Joyce

The Unfinished

We hold these truths to be self-expressive—

Though we dream in ordinary pants & are fulfilled
Though what we desire proves larger than mirrors
& Is aslant, like summertime
Dreaming in aslant cities, where every birth is unfulfilled

Although corrected by angles
On the self-explosive verge where cities fail
Dead like summer in yellow mirrors
& A lovely light is burning up the scourge

We think differently in heat, she told me once
Lopsided in a hall of mirrors like a cartoon swirl
Blurring the motions of onlookers
Burning the emotions which can only be imaginary

Burning up the palaces the emotions the cartoon world
At rest & even burning boring plots with sincere burning
Blurring the distinction between the readymade & the foregone
Burning up the image or the image on the page

Burning up the page
Burning up the here & later
Burning up distinctions which are also readymade
Burning up the page

The Unfinished

We can collapse mazes when we share the same breath

We can take Acheron to hell & turn it into a happy garden

We can look into each other's eyes & see the planet's history

We can sing like thrushes & cultivate rupture

We can invent the velocity of seeming to be still

We can thread spoken music in the pulse of failed cities

We can hear an engine's lungs

We can be the children our children will imagine

We can dart through intricate tree-fort worlds

We can believe that not having Paris is part of the fun

We can study the shapes of despoiled sea urchins

We can write novels in the sand & vote for our mothers

We can hear the laughter of the ocean

We can become whatever the full moon dreams of

We can whisper in decibels at which cathedrals dissolve

We can consider the rhizomic in the construction of themeparks

We can decimate bridges in order to rebuild them

We can wear the reflections of troubled outsiders

We can become the cause of the madness of bees

We can get tattooed with André Breton's "L'Union Libre"

We can investigate desire

We can insist on forever at a minimum

We can trouble the velocity of hummingbirds' shadows

We can be liminal & boundless when we speak, until

We are bound to the necessity which only love reinvents

[8] How much of this is private? Can our ideals affect singing? I have remembered to keep this silence, like some precious metal, between us. Ideas express inertia that we do not fear. Do we fear moving closer? Becoming the instability of description without seeming. I want you to describe what songs feel like. To upload the etymology of trippiness on a quiet morning. To rumble in the foyer of aloof trees. To explain how presence lingers even after departure. To recognize in me your childhood ghosts, haunted by untapped futures.

[9] Like all footnotes to nonexistent texts, I know how clouds must be. I would like to come crashing into your vocabulary like the smiles, or similes, of ghosts. Where noon isn't rectified until that sentence I forgot goes here. Grows outward, & then disappears. In the genius of slipping, like noon's erect factures, magnanimous as thinking out loud.

[10] To refer to others' desires, keep on thrashing. It was intense, at the outline of private departure. Although I seem to mitigate my position darkly as daydreams parade. Do we dare to hum or swell like forests' ghosts, thinking out of tune. It was too clear to mean anything, as hymns also grow impure in the retelling. Yet we toggled out of range & ate all the grace notes— and these younger nuns will still not bear it.

The Unfinished

Yet this is finished. That all that fullness

Could implode, when seizure is not reached

& We are what we have never felt

Being understood now as part of the critical

I understand, & would go back

Or forward, where this is not blown up

Yet this is, or was, something exultant

Without measure— not about you but about

Our ideals, except for one thing pivotal

As this is still or nothing without

Breath allowed as sheared, or shared

In noticed moments' exaltations

Upon thinking what about was or is captured

Intricacies of birds' shapes rising

Hacked, actually, in specific twists

The person was composed of chance expenditures

Lacking 'we' in our rotation

To render an invisible bird grammar

To count the earth's divisible joy at midnight's particles

To partition coming by Joycean means

To easily flare up where we both see

That this is nothing, writing

At the plainsong frisson of what could be critical

Although we nightly are coterminous with what is sung

Being part of the infinite

& The ridicule, & the look of it

Toward which we two divide when we

Are one; & this is still not done—

The Unfinished

If you plunged my heart into a river

Like Jeanne Moreau plunged

Into a river in that movie

Which is not lyric poetry in the age of Guantanamo

But is more like memories which collect across

An image of what still is lost

If you plunged   a river into my heart

It would not be a river of executive privilege

Like we said, there are no rivers

Only detours & historical circumstance

Which you don't understand since you weren't born in what we said we meant

& There is no here impressed upon your fingertips

Are there fingertips after the age of Guantanamo

Is there touch eroding privilege

Until we know that noon has settled into dusk

Just as in that movie which has been called lyrical

Both men who have their hearts broken are also soldiers

To remind us that even love is still barbarism   If you

Plunge   my heart into that river

Which is the river in the movie in the dreams we aren't having

In the age of Guantanamo, at which we aren't culpable

Lacking historical evidence in the poem which does not say anything

But drowns out the conventions of speechlessness

Where we still aren't implicated because this is too private

& Lyrical, in the at-risk noise

At the dearth of night where everything's teeming

& We still aren't here— & there were never feelings

Implicated   our session is over

In the historic silence lost against noise

At which everything we need is lost, but touch, which has not lasted

BOOK II.

For nothing started

No, that is not it at all. What we hunger for embodies rapture. A sad passage equally delayed. Who are fools inside the knowing without rupture. Without understanding what our heirs suspect. That every portion of a dream carries equal weight. That only fools renounce their birthright windlessly. That only real poets are so foolish to suspend a birthright which carries the weight of kings. That I am/am not a real poet. That you are not here to reason with this. And that we are both fools.

The Unfinished

Like thinking under your skin
When the song hurts
Still erect, but foregrounding
Some logic of transitional reply

Is still not private— the earth devours
This, this thing as yet unbroken
Invaded, in all public landscapes
Toward which we are in flight

To have been a nun in a former lifetime
Is not to grow quiet painting disappeared fishermen
Under the abandoned cities
Like some logic of transitional reply

Imagine another fucked-up noise
At which schemes are somehow blown wide open
Although I have lost my most prescient noise, this ghost—
The window of where I leave you behind

The Unfinished

We could extract this language in a cup

& Celebrate with ghosts only to find them reborn

As targets of blank history, soundbytes

Emptied of all silence

Is meaning embedded in fleeing?

The particulate in inattention

Filled up rapidly in the elated data

To have occurred there pivotally   is also 'real'?

As real as all official lies (can these

Be part of our investigations, now

The future is 'reborn'?

The imaginary a palpable bumpersticker

Where we are staged— if not finite

Prone, in fact, to diverse stimuli

At all points toward instigation slipping—

What is tomorrow? What is goodbye?

[11]Now that you no longer drink my sleep, I can read instead of waking. Night as a form of hunger. Where you are my ghost, dear crackpot. Easily in dreams where clouds sway us. Writing as a form of piracy which devours wakefulness. Even in the gaps where we aren't sure. It's not as easily said as what I meant in private. In the piracy of your evaporating tenderness. Nothing is as transitive as desire. For it is "the unfinished," you quipped, smilingly. Permanently changing the tune.

[12]I could say, *we should mean it* & disperse this logic. Transitionally against itself— to thrust or inflict a night pattern on what's accrued at the edges of goodbye. Strangled unlike characters. To reverse what angels mean.

[13]Some coffee spilled. Wind interspersed with the need to coincide with objects. To rush past what was faulted logically (though logic's not the point). To rush past what was lost, or brushed against. Interference with standstills.

[14]The point, dear oracle, has to do with slipping. Inconveniently past the point where cities weave. Slipping at the outset in order to drown out these coordinates from which the poem is transported. We knew everything before we started, had forgotten all before we were through. To be an instance of what was crushed. To be laterally outside these voices. As we create the distractions which inform our sleep. As we move to the threshold of what disappears ~~disapproves~~. This is not a narrative of its tropes but a disappearance into them. To reappear, fully formed, transparent, at the far side of desire.

[15]A city then, which is still unnamed.

The Unfinished

Without seeming to provide other examples

After the changes that rang

Although I would not pretend this seems

Exclusive. Desire to swallow the intimate

This is or will not swerve extended

Like the disk that will not play

Or pry intricate shambles from the maze of the popular

Until the blanks exhibit a kind of fucking

Which has been thrown against museums

Or thrust into livingrooms where the republican vice

Presidential candidate becomes an index of

Discourse by newsbyte puffery

To have an opinion not sampled, but equal

Upon brinks where liars swerved

The Unfinished

Whenever I read   a writer

      Refer to 'the reader'

I immediately think

    Of myself

        As someone else

•

In the strain of words which build

          Against examples

The cities were placeholders for transitional desires

Which break down ~~biodegrade~~

       In the geometries of love's lost need

•

You 'invent' whispering though I can't talk

Can't grow maddened at the unsunny
Barrage with things uplifted

•

Like the social explosive   outside of soldiers

Lost

Or everything else you would still fall down on

•

In the strain of worlds which

Build against explosions

•

"We're both poets, so we

Have the same

Religion"

The Unfinished

This occurs outside of fiction
Birds missing in relief

Bereft of midnight without
Touch

In spaces which we occupy

At the drama of what feels rational
Speech ruptured under
Laptop screens

At the center where
What's stirred
By midnight trembles

At the point where I'm serious I said I should stop

At the point where nothing

Returns ~~but to be rendered into light~~

•

Is there a *here* where the air repeats?
Forged outside of breath

It was not enough that they knew   that they knew

This feeling of having been occupied

Can you experience what resemblance feels like?

Operators & dispatchers are also sought

In the dream I was alone, but down by the palms

Experience was (still) not needed

To unfinish what was also stoked

Meaning   caught in the throat

The Unfinished

Above

The fields

Of things

Unwritten

Or likely

To get

Written

This gainful

Problem

Floated

In common

Neon

Affecting

Whispers

The crash

Of dull

Surprise

To have dreamed

of other differences

when days flew past:

one yellow, one calm

as nettles, one

extremely resistant to

barrage. Can scorched

dreams affect that

barrier? We will be

looking in on what while

appearing nonexclusive?

Appearing is also

appealing (& vice-

versa). To explode

the demands of

harbingers, already

written into night.

———

He was shameless. Drenched in the night-problem
without sucker punching. Without flickering
material at the pogrom tacitly readymade ~~if not
fleshly~~ if not having been molested. If not having
been anything at all— an analog to night where
grievers stood. After having written in the problem,
yet still understanding nothing of which we think
critically. Or anything, a surcharge, the cusps of
new demands we're too embedded to supply.
Folded in the blowout— in what's still not real, but
missing.

The Unfinished

Days become days while also we
Ratchet up the partial
Like daylight's dizzy edge
The caesura in pure desire
Two SUVs mating at a distance of correlative
Leisure, in the
Afternoon that's filling up

What's public initially seems easy
The direction of roads is certain
We can locate the direction of what's risked
But naming agitates regions
Of implied dreaming
An architecture prospective of the tongue
Counted at the edge of wind and shadows

'm not necessarily claiming to have been there. Trapped inside these faces. Nothing aims at us when we don't seem. Private as in violent. Trapped inside a gradient cinema, on an imaginary outline. Where we too have this 'crazy energy' as we invent a recombinant vocabulary in which there are no citizens. No employers or employees exchanging positions without character. Only children rushing in who dread this exposure. Listening to night— a system we don't believe in or deserve.

The Unfinished

To invert the mechanisms of untrapped sleep

At which tomorrow is fulfilled

A dead being, or product placement

      Who wreck their cars in private

Or are driven to expend

To wreck their cars, o unwashed citizens

You catalogue of freaks

I am entangled with you as with

      Someone else

Who forever scorched my sleep

- - - - - - - - - - - - - - - - - - - -

Orpheus was fulfilled, unlike Vallejo[1]

---

[1]Poetry is for losers

Baudelaire   Vallejo   Spicer   Berrigan

Every one destroyed

By sins of his own naming

The Unfinished

When energy fails, you will not think
In the attractions without charge

You think you knew them elsewhere
Without age, without voice

These things we sing out loud
Don't fear us

The energy is in the body
Blooming when we speak

The Unfinished

What, in utter

Desecration lays

    A leaf, or general

Economy

   ~~Dominion of~~

Encases strange

  "Lip service" trumpets

         strumpets

   enclosing for the general

Features of

     wind, is all

Or neither ~~smother~~

       proportions   lay

  each unto   Other

Each to whom

      I had forgotten, were

   speaking

        forgotten whirr

Of (dis)closure

      cleft & rattle

  penmanship & guardingly, guardingly rail

My summer (ample) gardens

         stunners

   Box of each

      compulsively—

The Unfinished

1.

The muted particulars are also free

To swim in intermediate attention

To the left of the enlarged texts which also swarm

Or swarm as if rapidly to overtake hunting

A 'marquee experience' a curve beside lakes

Toward which to place what feels

Exclusive now that winter's going forward

Going into something driven free

To feel to free to flee to feel

This up & feel this uses up the night

This useless ghost-image becoming experience

Being done with ghosts & those who see them

Or those who have seen winter ride away

& Her cloak trailing leaving

Behind a kind of private outcome

For robust Spring to decide

2.

That the tongue is abler than the mind

'Speak for yourself' is like a diamond

Though cloudy, & the sun engages

World's weight, or the weight of winter

The weight of winter now is seizing up

                              the first

The earliest moments of spring

                                 We ascend

& Engines gorge on smoke & billowing

Earth. We can't see the horizon in this light

Not twilight, but darkly

                                 resonant ~~resistant~~

The mind resists poetry, but does the tongue

Or mind, in its deeper recesses

                                     billowing

      Lavish it?   ~~Ravish it?~~

Let's see if it finishes language   the poem   this earth

Forever in a state of disappearing

              Intransitive, disappeared—

3.

It might be smoke, but I don't know

& Yet it isn't. To want them, lavishly

      As any reflection

Of a tongue or noon

          Is trapped, in gathering night—

My page isn't wide

Enough, for my lines (I write large)

        ~~(I write to enlarge)~~

To feel better that it's burning

                Is to see

The specific weight of the line, or noon, or night

Their resistances spinning

Outside or inside

A residue, a context—

Is like saying

"Oh, he wrote that   because

He wanted to   write

Something called 'The Unfinished'"

& Hold it, bodily—

The Unfinished

Logos as transitive

      What I see in air
Stops turning

      Rife with suspects
        ~~The infinitive a~~
        ~~Careless threshold~~

To speak of these
      Things bodily

At the point where we
      Don't leave—

•

      To take

      The leap

      Between the

      Serious &

      Dead

      Weight of

      Birds, a

      Come-hither

      Variety &

      Scale of

      What

      I realize

      I don't

      Need

That the body encompasses what
Doesn't bleed—

& That we are here, in hindsight

•

We can accept him-or-her as
What it wants.

We can accept fine details of accretion

Accumulation is American logic

I am, or am not, on standby

It is interrupted now, & all right here

Interspersed by marginal details of nightfall

Dictation as transitive   desire

The pen is crushed by ligatures

Swirling on the page

Anything less than the pale horizon

Except in pure lines, which hindsight doesn't form

The Unfinished

It is dead. & We accomplished nothing

            I had thought
            What that moment would
            Be, when it
            Happened.

The strain of looking. of saying, & not
Really

We are dead to each   ~~after such atrocities~~
                  ~~as the world knows, what does it really~~
      Other   ~~matter?~~

This silence which speaks everything
Speech, which renders nothing

          Goodbye, Dear Almost

      My most cutting equation

BOOK III.

For reason & wild surprise

The Unfinished

If it's dead, I killed it.
Then am I
A murderer of ghosts?

Do memories leave
The body—
Or become transported

& To whom would you
Address these forecasts
If there are no ghosts

Only ghostly immediacy
Beastly silence
Undone by gathering light

•

There is something you need which you
Don't use.

Not a ghost, but a duplicate
Memory (crowds pierced

By glancing
Machines)—

To mistake
A kind of brotherhood

For the subject of this
Sentence

In windows' dreams where we
Aren't real

~~& To be inducted by~~
~~This silence~~—

Ancient less than still.

•

The edge is different at the outline
There are no more words

At the ancient edges of machines
The machinery is unwritten

Elsewhere. Where we
Are also spoiled ~~spilled~~ —

Its careless ghost a kind of brotherhood
Lacking births which young men's dreams fulfill

emember when the lights went out? Will it ease your expression? As a crayon or pantaloons trashed at the onset. Of what? You like to ask questions. That's because answers seem dubious. It depends who is listening. To smoke a crayon like guests in questioning. An image of pants split down the middle. Anyone can say this, but no one has. To sing, this is obvious. A precarious listening. To document the guacamole (or something more serious). I still don't know who is listening. Spicer asked this first. To become pummeled with questions, or harbingers. Or else to get split down the middle. Who can say? Who's on first? A steady assignment. New pants, different ballgame. Although I am still omnivorous as tomorrow. Although I cannot hear myself whispering. Or you, speaking your voices, of which I already told you in private. Ever? Again?

The Unfinished

To keep going as a means

    To find out what we

What

  We didn't have

      To say

In spaces where we dance

    Become popular

In the spaces where the worlds

  Inquire

A feeling becoming noise becoming

    Necessary to say

Is necessary

  When you finish any work, it is

Born again in a new form ~~firm~~

  Blurred in private, like my

     Dance

A particular recovery ~~reverie~~

   Becoming stable in the

  Silence like tomorrow

The spaces of, &

   Which intrinsic

Dare me to sing, at a panic

  Something

Least intrinsic or purported

   Are you here?

Can I burst this likeness?

  Mandatory like a stammer

An intrinsic way of looking

        This becomes you like the air itself

James Joyce disliked the look of

            Quotes

     I like the look of common suggestion

The air in particular

       Its unfinished gaze

Seeming to move outside

         The angle

    Of vision of incessant cities

      Which all draw past

In blasted reflection

     Burnt inside the work becoming

The work (again) in turn—

The Unfinished

The first is also the hardest

   Point

       At the windows of the edges where we speak

Where we sing, it was a twist

    Is past. Is also what we

Feel / Felt / Fell

    Off, or out of the cold,

       Cold morning

The morning was awake

    The light was striated

It was teeming

It imbues us in the way

    Clothing covers a body

   Or parts of several

Bodies

    To lean

Against the outlines of cities, with faces

    Streaming past

(The faces are not clothed, usually)

Where it is particular, & still not summer

& Any look seems possible

To regain the exact mention of desire

     While universes cling

   To our hair

& We are stopped, as at a fruitstand, wanting to

      Eat the papaya

     Rank with sweetness

The weather in uniform opposites
        Being sunny & rainy at almost the same
Breath
                Wildflower sprigs in your hair, it is
June it is tentative   concurrent like flowers
        Like flowing it is
A speech that no one listens to
                Being June itself
Lush like the outlines of what quivers
                        There is
                Touch but no relief as
The wind flaps, & rain
        Hovers impossibly
Patient before falling
        In whispers broken
Off like sprigs
        Of June in your nightflung hair
Being air, or night apart
        From song, or apart from being sung
Or from being sung to sleep
Or from hair in your teeth or the tenderness
                Of strangers
Or the laughter of breath in the snow
        Which doesn't exist yet (do you exist?)
Or your eyes, or the tune of night's drifting
Or your eyes your brown blue
        Grey green eyes which pierce me
Which unsettle waking   make me not sleep

The Unfinished

It is the ongoingness which catches
Me. Days come & go, much like another,
Usually.   Poems also
    Catch on each other
Like lovers in the other's
        Hair
Each alike   but yet
The persistent outlines of the trees
    We invent, as if by voice
Until the immediacy stops (does it
        Stop?) Love
Reinvents what it does not need.   It
    Doesn't. This is still (not) true. The
World beguiles us with its slinging
    We invent rash, paper copies
Of our understandings, partial
        As the skyline, seen
Through a window. We
Are diverted when we are
        Diverted.
It's terrible, though it's still not Sunday
History speaks through the crevices
Distortions pile up.
        Would I love you if you wore
That jacket? Would any of these
Things matter
        In another tongue, with different trees
        Swaying in moonlight?

[16]Education's unconsumed. Driven into night like rain. If I consume this thing, perhaps I am overthinking the situation. Reaching into the assembly. To piece the language shreds into a body. An idle threat or substance, derived from irregular breathing.

[17]It is birthed through active range. Exceeding a reaction to what's not grasped. To litter in brilliant distortion's ravishing. Through effigies of sunlight cracked. The effigies are for what you forgot you knew. For what was lost, until thrashed awake in raiments which consume the flesh of written stillness.

[18]To be capable of wounding oneself deeply. Deeply enough in order to see. To sear in a rhythm or mention. To sing reactively, to the silence of words thrashing. To be utterly destroyed in knowing. To speak, when necessary— & do so retroactively at a moment's surge.

The Unfinished

Like ghosts who sit delicately

Like ghosts who are a trope for being shattered

Like ghosts who have some terrified religion

Like ghosts who have a license not to strut

Like ghosts who are as terrified as I

Like ghosts who don't say 'lowghost' while thinking of Jack Spicer

Like ghosts who do not think of elsewhere, or Jack Spicer

Like ghosts ~~I told you not to think~~

Like ghosts who thrive at the edges of goodbyes

Like ghosts who don't pick up the phone

Like ghosts still unafraid of elsewhere

Like ghosts who manifest themselves as sea urchins

Like ghosts now sucking on the real

Like ghosts who shrink outside of intermediate machinery

Like ghosts now acclimated to such sorrow

Like ghosts who often sway

Like ghosts who swarm at impossible religions

Like ghosts now almost with no clothing

Like ghosts who sometimes aren't exquisite

Like ghosts who sing, unafraid of neon

Like ghosts somewhere off the page

Like ghosts who are insurgents at the written moment still not forged

The Unfinished

The blank page is relentless

It swallows this, it bores inside you

Until we hold up night

Outside its field of vision

Becoming that which young men breathe

Until its edges fray

Here we are, being animals

Have you taken the roof off the lake?

To dream of what casts no reflection

Written into light

•

The blinding light coincides with itself

To be blinded, one must have a body

Intermingled with whispers

It is the dead, sitting here

Emitting neon screams of which we now

Can't talk

•

To be ghosts, while lacking dullness
Frightening the patrolmen away
Whose odd support defaces buildings'
Shadows

To have been done in by former lifetimes
Coincides with the forbidden
Becoming that which young men dream
Until its edges sway

•

The blank page dreams the forbidden
Being written into night

The Unfinished

To drown this conceit, & the putting together

& This sense of what gets lost between

What constructs & *is*

Constructed— actor & acted

Upon. The earth rises

To meet your step?

We have also felt this way

When we are here, & buildings change us

Change the relations of light to objects

Which cities would erase

Being unconstructed

Adrift in the real, & the putting together

As city is to night— as desire to its transient structure

While we are also being dreamed

The Unfinished

To have no vocabulary for this hunger
Makes it unsayable? What is sayable?
The air gently moves. Where
Does it come from? What force
Drives it? Is it

We who have no vocabulary
Or is there an *it* we are not
Saying? If we are not, then is it
Unsayable? Would the air,
If it stopped moving, no longer be air?

What fool knows this weight
Of unspokenness— this turning about
As breath not vocalized? If breath's not
Vocalized, where does it die? If thought's not
Fleshed, where is it devoured?

To have, but not, a fleshly vocabulary
For these coincidences, this turning about
Inside the visible but just outside the spoken,
The spokes of the turning, & the flesh & the air it
Consumes. What good to even have a vocabulary

If we don't use it, even to whisper

This thing, this unspoken? What good to

Have flesh, & to touch (yes, to touch casually)

If not to give oneself wholly to the weight,

The gravity of touch— if one

Holds back meaning this thing & the weight of it?

Given wholly to form. If we are

Given holy to form, would it drive us mad—

Incapable of speaking, of putting words

To the thing we mean but cannot name,

To the touch we ache but cannot breathe?

If we, who use breath to move air,

To vocalize, to imagine, are so bare,

So fearful to even say, to touch, to

Bear the world at brim—

Until speech isn't even necessary.

after Creeley

The Unfinished

But if you *say* anything, it implicates passage—
The specific positions of animals,
& We in our animal bodies.
Animals do not have feelings.
I don't; I have killed them.
As the rain comes rushing
Toward what
End? The saying & the
Being of animals. It complicates the social
Through which we are still rushing
Past, always rushing
Past. The
Past is complicated—
A hybrid of social & animal
Necessity. I shall install it
In a cabinet, so that I may look at
It from time
To time.
Afterwards, I shall name this urge, this
Surcharge, this ceaseless motion.
Titles complicate desire.
People implicate those they are next to;
In this way we are like poems.

The Unfinished

To say embodies ghosts.

    To mean or leave radically

In a room you are ~~not~~ leaving

Or sitting— haunted

      But to name, in radical structures

The structures also notice ghosts

    Who are

Not sitting. Being embedded in a structure, you

Or we, as persons in a statement

      (To be embalmed, imagined vertically

While also being unfulfilled—

•

To move in summer, or outside of buildings.

This is not a statement; there are

Things in it; it is here, or summer—

A condition being dreamed

•

To move in summer, just outside of buildings

        With faces going past:

*The tune is shattered. It was breaking up the phone. Estrangement is a
virtue of the wicked. This feeling of enclosure complicates desire. It is
here, in spelled rhythms. This is lame. I want inanimate desire, but if
it's not wherever then swallow the partitions. Strike that; I want—*

•

What Spicer meant by dictation is not to write until it's necessary.

•

Poems birthed of desire   ~~speed~~

Where the wicked are still free

[19]To be disruptive while also starving. ~~Staring into night.~~ In this fabulous disarray where we aren't sure. At the slender edge of no relief. Where nothing which is real is also spoken. These are segments of dreams (not popular). Like the edges of imaginary bodies. Yet I'm too aloof to keep remembering until it pierces breath with what comes later. But to keep remembering in imprints, in imaginary outlines. Who kisses in the conditional tense will grow impermanent as smoke.

[20]No man, but a boor, ever wrote, except for passion. To be inside what's also forged against relief. At the tender ledge, or edge, where music frays. To dream in offkey music, inventing fascination. Or forge anything which can hinge on lost but disembodied vocals.

[21]Transition of nothing which traces breath to act. Near winter's stillest hour, where we surge. The body somehow mandates the popular. To lurch by tangible samples of what's aimed. Dreams are examples of transitional data. To fold in air while we don't smoke. To whisper as if to cut off noise (whispers that fill up with night).

[22] *"There is no boundary dividing life from art."* —Jerome Rothenberg, Reading, 6/23/09.

The Unfinished

But naming can also mean vanishing—
A hook invented on which to hang
What we no longer can
Conceive of

•

In the wind, with flowers thrashing—

•

There is a sudden voice. There is
A picture wrapped in
Structure

There is a clairvoyant image or surcharge—
Depth of night
Depth of night

•

Notice that I didn't populate
The distance between fleeing & perceiving,
Being embedded & the capacity
(Not) to touch—

•

Venetian Cream. Bronze Skull. Akron,

Ohio. Bucharest. Lucy in the Sky with

Diamonds. William of Orange. William Carlos

Williams. USA Today. John Neon.

Eleanor Roosevelt. Southern Hemisphere.

Kansas. American Idle. Darfur. West

Bank. Sarajevo. Ciudad

Juarez.—

•

The way a camera captures

A speaker, people

Passing on the street behind her

The way reflection, mirroring,

Distorts

& Colors change in differing light

Evaporating in plain sight

Depth of night

Depth of night

The Unfinished

Evaporating in plain sight
                       Under what

Night gathers.

Night gathers surfaces.

Night gathers surfaces' smittenness.

Like last night after Maureen read, the full

Moon over red

        Lights & gold-

Lit clouds

        Which daylight clarifies. Nothing

Is as full as we are, of its dark

             Wildness. The surface

Is an idea which does not clarify

                  Night.

We are in love with our ideas, though.

We are in love

        With the surface

           Appearances of the world

& Clouds. We are in love with our own dark

Revolvings. Dark like night. Dark like

The fucking, & the wanting to be fucked.

Dark like light. The inner surface which

The world pries apart. A part of this is teeming.

I am The Surface, a character in this

Play. I am what you constantly wait for,

        Being unfulfilled.

I am the park with dark inner light.

I am the parting, & the wanting to be torn.

I am what is not finished, when you

          Can say this. Above

All, I am what you cannot say—

That we are real as smoke;

That lightning strikes, but not just once;

That it is the forbidden that we yearn for;

That we dare not speak, when we speak;

That, controlled by cycles too, we adore moonlight;

That what you think of cycles is reductive;

That being is materially unfulfilled;

That the night or its dark

               Registers gather silence;

That love is not destroyed, but takes new shape

          Dispersing as all matter into sight.

The Unfinished

Dispersing as all matter into sight—

Light, the immediate

Bodies to deflect sensation

& We, unimaginable

    As a lipprint on tinderbox a chinese

Curtain a residue

    & Angels who come to mind bodily

We are intermediate in our dislocations

We are aligned with evidence of frantic bodies

    I don't know why it's like this   sensations

Of light applied to tangible

Bodies

But still addressed to matter & to light

Addressing itself to matter in plain sight

To the up-in-the-air moment intersected

    By teeming

Taken in as all intersected stride

Mistakenly as night, or air, consumes us—

•

Breathless now in lucent grasps

Tattooed or familiar

An edge of makeshift crashing, driven

Outside of which all light is hunger—

    Fateful, unconsumed

•

What does not scream is lost in attention

What is lost is fragile surface torn apart

Brutal gesture

As full as tomorrow, where we are guests, gesturing

Bloody screams for the ghost in tomorrow

The Unfinished

When I say it will not bloom, it will not

 Bloom. The sky comes apart graphically.

The geography of desire is unstable

 As June's sudden storms. She is a sudden

Storm—

   Flash, & then gone.

The Unfinished

When I say it will not bloom, I mean to
   Tear up this rainy   suddenly July
Afternoon, & start over, &
   Over in air, burning—

I mean to. But it will not ring.
   & The *sung* precisely is unreliable
& Integument, the parted

     It drifts over meaning like smoke. This noise
What of it? I am a stable variety
   A seriously unstable contingent
The absence of which is smoke.   I am not

I am, nor am I, increasingly swiftness
   Of tongue & whatever else is night.
A swiftness in the varieties of buildings & gardens
   Against which nothing has been rung.

    (There are men, old
    Or middleaged, walking
    The park with barely their
    Wits
    About them)—

•

How are these pressed

    Intonations viable?

Where the flora are outnumbered

      & Would sink

Into counted circum-

      stance. There is a train

Or positions of bodies restlessly—

    Bodies there or

Numb with desire—

      Or numb with forgotten

        Desire.

Desire is the rose the dangerous quantity the

    Position on the map which burns our

Eyes.

      Our eyes were here to be sated.

   I am scratching out your breath.

The heat continues, dumbly—

    As you or I or anyone

Could trace this breath to its core—

Your core.   Our core.   Your core.

The Unfinished

Toward haunted as we wish we get

Could be leaving & partial

As brittle heat wildly   We are all

     Seemingly here or haunted

As the sun out there

In positions of the night in traffic

     Placed together— being dissimilar

As the wind intrinsic or flinching

Through dark orders of unwritten sky

     The sky is written in your

Retinas— reflected here

     In the sun thick with noon

& The cries of passing strangers

Delicately out of tune—

BOOK IV.

For what gets lost

How can I make it disappear— this burden of naming? Of assigning weight to what's not sizable. Of measuring what is still not told.

Thinking ruptures its own boundaries. As with being human ~~shattered~~. To be a red-light yoyo or the whims of fools. Like desperados who agitate to be consumed in fleshly guises. Gainsaying the visible, or the outlines of the visible.

Footnotes are for fools without memory. To be without memory is to be continually reborn. Or silent; or the King of Fools. The poet-fool swallowing his own reflection in pages which evaporate. The reader catalyzed, changed but useless, among words which are chronically erased. As Monk's performance of Ellington is superimposed with noisy car alarm down there, where there is no thief. Is noise the thief, or is it this false necessity of naming?

Then what is necessary? Is it is only to be entertained/ entranced? & Is this true of poetry as of elsewhere?

To cast off those whose broken reflections make carbon cities disappear. If it's true I don't want to use it. As I don't want to own anything that's rare, or shrill, or beautiful. Don't bother me, darling, until I'm liable for this image, & the other, the one I'm still not sure of. I remember being a teenager, walking gangly streets in a bright city where no one bled. To swallow your name, your tender abrasions, while still refusing to become anyone I would vote for (if I had no choice). ~~Do we have a choice, dear townspeople?~~ & To still vote tenderly, for a mouthful of words. If only it were still that easy— to bleed or to withdraw.

The Unfinished

Here is the Book with its

Excesses—

Exhausting all proportion

Until the sun comes up

Because I still don't know if I am ready

I'm ready, but I still don't know

& Believe we must give way

& Believe we certainly must now sway

We must now all give away

With emotions

All blown

Past

~~In past is rest~~

All poems are finished

In the span it takes

For a glance or hand

To reach its end. Until all else is shrill

Confection—

The mind at rest,

Or the body at liberty.

The Unfinished

It's night & you are not asleep
Though ghosts cling to your hair
Making summer still more real
Whom we would often blur

In the echo, in the allure
Flashing ligatures
Clasped like shadows still not captured
Bendable as straw

Then to rise out of the earth like laughter
Which our thinking selves repeat

The Unfinished

To still come out the other side

    Free of all positioning

        Dumbly where stars meant

To capture

        If they fell, or we

    We, in plangent

Mention— in swift

    Occurrence of such time

        Of tune, unswiftly seeming, but going—

When you go, you are in

          Motion (wasted?)

    Delicately out of tune

& The steps it takes to get there—

    Are they gone too?

        Then it's just you, or singly

No longer being here

    Where is here, or are

    This tenuous

        Edge of being &

Saying

    Swiftly, swiftly to go

            Past

In past is rest. In here, incess-

    antly *potential*—

Time is the placement of very small things

      Keep in time

    Is my timing off?

Off of what? This place?

    What is this place, & how

  Was I *placed* here? *Am I*

        Here, or only

            To re*place*

Transitions' ghosts— some gutted

    Impact?

       & The trees, over here—

  Raindripping, shaggy—

       Time, too, is their enemy,

Evoked in pirate

    Instances like

      Sleep

  Toward which the dead give way—

  Get on your mark

Can you outrun

      Swift-fallen days—

Landscape stealing motion—

    & This gravity which seals us

      In

  Positions ever blurring?

DEHSINIFNU EHT

Today is porous with material

I eat the future

Its long legs encircle me, sometimes

What will I say to tomorrow?

My shorts are full of noise

I can no longer hear this vanishing

•

The reversal of this image dreams a future which is already erased. Deflected into thunder which you cannot smoke. Where light grows irregular. There is a torsion under your lips which will not keep still. Cannot possibly bloom, until I see you in this light. For *light* insert *night*. An endlessness forged at stray edges of the tongue. The better to sing your name.

•

When I look into mirror, I am often somewhere

Else. Days flew past

When I look into mirror I am elsewhere, between

Here & the edges of what sings

•

What sings is currently at a table

It does not have much time   it flees this

It flings this

The shiny restlessness of cities ghosts this space

It is a shiny cartography

A jackpot foolishness   a residue

Which the new implodes in cities while we wake

•

The light goes out behind the mirror

Everything sings

Which is unreflected

Inflected on our tongues

Our eyes reflect

What does not b(l)ind us

While we wait we are not sung to

In the mirror which uncovers silence

When the wind grows blank

To be these instances where we don't dream

To uncover whispers under cities

As the days grow long, & no one whispers

A private landscape.   A subjective barrage.

The Unfinished

for Chuck Pirtle

At the double edge of being & saying

Writing these lines in order to free them

Where the structure of the night is tuneless

& I want to eradicate the edge between pages

& The light that runs away

To make of the body an emblem

Drenched in smoke

To make the skin between poem & world—

The life around it & 'inside life'—

Porous with new meanings

To flee like smoke while the wind runs away

At the edges of a daylight wrapped in structure

Tuneless with new poems which slip

Onto pages & outside them, &

The light that runs away

Containing the skin & its meanings &

The pages of the night which are not tuneless

Outside of emblems' tragic smoke

Which slips beside the days that we

Erase to make new days or pages (only to be devoured in turn)

The Unfinished

Ideally, it should cause a swoon

A rupture in composure

A contemporary negation zone

A novelty, pleasant company

Will we get past resistance to

Ideas? What will make you sing?

The structure of a parkinglot, a recipe

For soup, the economics

Of deforestation— any

Of these can be investigated.

If you stumble, get up.

If you're blocked, learn to see

Everything for the first time ever.

Cause a stir, resistance

To old roles. Write, in the hardness

Of language's rustling.

Burn your writing till you mean it.

Complicate desire.

The Unfinished

When I look into
　　　　Mirror, I see
So much more that should be
　　　　　Visible—

Breath dividing
　　　　Self from other
Selves—

Reflecting shadows which form no ghost

　　　Ghost, the double of the critical
　　　　Subtracting leaf from object

At imperfect distances we would deface

　　　A tension or possibility
Which the wind repeats
　　　In our erotic confusion.

　　　　The balance is the forbidden:
That which is erased—

　　　Ghosted in transparence;

Turbulence of the unseen

The Unfinished

Poetry, as I have said, is information

But information dissipates

& What is usable is still not bought

But increasingly given

Away, like poetry

Yet to still become all passionate display

Until what's rendered becomes pregnable

As smoke

Then to still become what's rendered, & give way

To all slinking dispossession

Which makes hindsight vulnerable

Until only the earth is private

Then to end up only with a mouthful of words

The Unfinished

To begin again with a mouthful
Of words where tongues meet
Tongues meet in edgy silence
To leave here speechless   reborn in light

& The light that runs away
Dragging worlds askew with jagged eyes
Where in solstice-light we are free
Are we? or merely beginning

Beginning & rebeginning
To be still undone by night's arrival
A carnival, incessant desire
Folded in the place where all tongues meet

Where cities are constructed (cities
Are constructed / conscripted / constricted
Constantly, unconsciously)
& We inhabit them like beggars

Wary of our destinations—
Of the light askew, but tripping up
The blind—
Or world that runs away

While cities multiply, unthinking

The Unfinished

Even if seeming to not sit still
Where the earth falls off, here, at the finished
Sentences, the composed mind, the orderly
Misperceptions.

Attention is ruly. Having been authorized
To speak. To stop. To start & then
Go off in solstice-light, in daylight, the visible
'Here' in air— the earth-infused

Stopping like a sentence-mirror above a gorge   ~~gap~~
Where this gaping is unseemly. It shows its seams
It necessitates breaks in   attention   action   plot
It breaks in when it wakes us   when it rhymes with doubt

It sets the mind akimbo to sit still
When the mind wants to be kinetic, & it warrants
Stutters, & effaces false   certainties & acts
Of inattention to *things* in their detail

To the heaving motion of things in
Their relations— their interlockings & un-
certainties,
Their drifts & embarkations. These

Shall refuse our finishing.

The Unfinished

How much of this is made
In whispers? Are there
Ghosts in traffic
Where the air is silent? Who

Designs our cities,
& How do they
Evolve? What mechanism
Drives this panic

Of streets whose names continually
Are erased?
Of highways gone in mad
Directions? So that to live's continually

To be erased. But how do *they*
Evolve? How do cities, like organisms,
Biologically
Behave? (There is

A difference between
Evolution &
Expansion— which seems
Lost on Americans.)

I myself got lost today
Three times, being
An American on a highway, gladly
Resolute & offtrack. But are

There ghosts? & Where is any
History in traffic—
Hurtling unquenched toward the 'new,' the
Next or any other

History or vacancy—
An uncanny, directionless surcharge—
& The voiceless *here*, all hurtling
Past—

The Unfinished

But to still come here in the unanswered questions

Within the unquestioned answer

Inflecting ghosts like daylight makes

All questions disappear.

If to appear's to air in silence fleeting

Fitting air where appearance is

Unguessed. Am I the ghost? Don't you

Know that? No

I see ghosts like old movies, on unfinished buildings'

Sides. I pray for old men. History

Is in a panic.

Like all highways against which ghosts don't

Run. Then is it we who are trafficked?

History's an apparition.

Hers too. Neither

Will admit it.

The Unfinished

I.

Is it we who are the trafficked,

Squandered by devices?

The interface deforms the sentence.

People have conversations with ghosts

But the new ghosts

Do not haunt us

The news ghosts swallow time;

They distract us.

People have conversations with themselves.

There is no history, no memory

There is the next thing, and the next, & the

Thing next, which

Effaces it.

II.

Here you are with your face at the door

I will teach you to whisper

To walk the earth casting no reflection

To become my ex-lover

To still devour silence

To stop outside careening time &

Be swallowed by devices

III.

To still cast no reflection

In the gaps outside of fire without thought

In the gaps outside memory

In the

They are ghosts because they are outside time

I still do not believe

The haunted & the image of the haunted

~~The hunted~~

Who move outside of images

We are overcome by images.

Their numbers swell, but their meaning isn't stable

Like poems

But unlike poems, they horde attention

Burning memories for fuel

IV.

The space between poem & the image

Is mediated by ghosts

The Unfinished

But to still be permeated
In worlds without tendering
Where the crossouts form

A line across
The body (the line is permeated
By geography, memory)—

A scrawled tattoo line,
A Kafka penal colony line,
Not a penile line (the line's not

Gendered).
Is language gendered by its
Users? Are we able to

Speak?
I speak, while also entering
The room (room which marks my meta-

phorical pretensions).
But somehow the room runs away
From me, & so I enter

Into unmarked space
Incessantly, restlessly—
To run away & drive us

Whole

Where cities evolve, in a maze of mirrors

& We dream of broken reflections

But still we are deformed by

Ghosts— ghosts who find us

Here—

What is it that you want me to say?

—To lie asleep, your tongue on fire.

—That was a serious question.

—And that a serious answer.

—What is serious? The world is comical.

—It's still important to see.

—See whom?

—And it. Or around whom? And into what?

—We cannot know. We know only that we are seeing it. Saying it.

—So seeing & saying are connected?

—It becomes impossible to speak to you, sometimes.

—But that was another serious question.

—Exactly.

—I think seeing & saying are all one.

—Be careful. The one is passive, the other reactive.

—No, both can be active, investigative, piercing. Just as there can be passive forms of talking. Speech which is merely reflex, or its own echo.

—To look might also be to examine.

—Yes, that's what I'm saying. And to say might also be a way of looking into the matter.

—Of thinking out loud?

—More, if it arrives on the spot.

—Then the trick is to land, but not be spotted?

—More to see, without letting light itself blind you.

—And to say what it is necessary to believe?

—What is necessary to believe is not quite true. Is this a paradox?

—Only if we need to resolve it. But what we are talking about applies equally to poets & philosophers & thinking citizens.

—Is there a difference?

—There's supposed to be.

—Says who?

—Consensus Reality, for starters.

—Anything about which consensus is needed is not reality proper— for example, the fact that that rock over there is hard. Therefore, such 'reality' is constructed— an ideology (though I dislike that word)— & the 'consensus,' in that case, is up for grabs.

—Then what about evolution? Global warming? These can be factually demonstrated, yet fall prey to the ideology *du jour*.

—That's because nobody understands science, including you.

—As nobody understands poetry, perhaps including me. Or philosophy. Or the plot of *The Big Sleep*.

—When things are not commonly understood, they become subject to distortion. To manipulation. This is the source of common skepticism toward scientific & poetic truth. Though the dissemblers often enough are the very ones who claim to doubt.

—Then you believe there is poetic truth ('poetic' not being in scare quotes)?

—Go ask Shelley.

—This is why you're so difficult to talk to! The public would say you're flip-flopping.

—I'm wearing boots, thank you very much. And the 'public,' so called, is unaware of anything but itself. I prefer another calling than to try to please it.

—Or please anyone. Is this elitist, or just advanced introversion? But you still haven't answered me about truth.

—Poetic truth? The poetic method, you'll recall, differs from the scientific. Actually, I was trying to be an Unacknowledged Legislator.

—How quaint.

—Yes, well we were talking about truth, & nothing could be quainter. Whose conceptualism is it, anyway?

—Perhaps I should have asked, do you believe in truth?

—Not 'Truth,' exactly. I believe what is the case. & Poetry is part of that.

—But does poetry create truths or uncover them?

—Neither. It embodies them.

—But what about the duties of poets?

—To set the mind at brim.

—But what's the use of it?

—You might as well ask that of art itself. Or of protected sex.

—Do we need protection, from art or anyone?

—From ourselves, sometimes. The human is really a darker animal than is generally admitted. But that is not currently part of the plot of this poem.

—Then this *is* a poem? That's what I was getting at.

—It is part of a fairly long poem, which now needs to go on.

—And so we're done.

The Unfinished

To hear it alternately where it does not run

Where it leaves, but does not disappear

Into light like winter

Into night, like sleep, jettisoned

By dreams of common things. To

Construct for us a city—

A pure location that we've filled the air with.

No mind is pure

Which cannot contain

Perversity— & yet,

There are traces of such things

As drive us mad, even

In the most intimate gesture.

What drives to *sense*—

The poem fallen

At the margins of the night.

Night which glows

In earthly silence—

Until no one speaks,

Even the dead.

The Unfinished

Hunger is a place, a scene

That's never written.

Then is the unwritten without

Mention, or erased?

It is an absenting, a

Vanishing— words

Ghosted off the page.

I never meant to dream

That city,

Or become corporeal in its absence.

Emptied of the dream, of what

Seems real, when cold air hits the page.

This light of not-being. Of not being

Human.

In this ghost-light, this absence

I shake the language.

Language, which bears

Fruit.

•

This is the Poem speaking.

Silence, too, is generative, says the Poem.

Only the noise, the white noise, shuts down meaning.

Naming is making. Isn't

Meaning, but its

Progenitor. It

Continues, then breaks down, but still

Goes forward. Is always going

Forward.

•

It

Is never finished.

Then the poem will not be? Someday.

I

Am just a human,

Vehicle for this language.

Language which bears

Fruit—

Poem, taking

Deeper roots.

The Unfinished

Written into seeming

    What we have

It goes on without us knowing

There is a song there. We have finished it

        Above the trees

Trees which seem oddly written

& In knowing, or clear light

It all stops. Stop this hunger

    This knowing, this erasure

Written still against the boundaries

        The sky

Growing dark now (we all grow dark).

Night is a form of hunger

    The written into folds

Of teeming

        Life (life without memory)

There is no memory because there are no roots

There are no ghosts, only news ghosts

There is no translation, only appropriation

There is no invention, only constant novelty

There is no death, there is moving to Florida

There are no foundations, because the architectures swarm

Crowding them out. Crowding us out.

Have you been crowded from this life?

I am cold, sitting here, erasing.

I mean from the life of the mind.

That's why I am cold.

You are cold because it is darkening winter.

The life of the mind keeps warmth away. Money to burn.

The crowd or crowding out.

It has as much to do with silence.

To go forward without novelty, but teeming.

Despite this noise. Noise which surrounds us. Shrouds us.

But forever to go forward—

The Unfinished

Until the purplish, imagined
    Rosy stars
Become more real, as real as night—
        A thing
In window looking inward;
Until the night becomes more real
     & Things are lucid to themselves,
          Are they begun
To shimmer, in erotic displacement.
      Then is all
Palpable to itself?
       Am I real
In the quick felt solid
    As nightfall, or the unfinished
Gaze of trees?
     & Our rosy selves, contiguous
         With real
      Or imagined voices, spilling
          Past—
To be here anyway, at the edge of elsewhere
     In ghosted cities, now
    Imperiled—
By the high
      Cost of weaving by
    Ghost images (which no one pictures)
In the silence of not being named.
       Of being un-named—
    Void of name & tongue, & the
          Ability to speak.
Then to speak, what now becomes more real
     In the voice, still not pictured—

The Unfinished

Look, here is no one pictured
All trouble reaching imagined futures
Until the stars don't disappear, they shirk
Don't spill across the ghosted

Dreams no one pictures (there are no
Pictures)
To fill the page with wages ~~wagers~~
Old men's stories. Nothing formed.

The page is consumed by light outside it
It evades speech. It does not strum
If the page tried to sing, would you hear it?
If the page disappeared, what would it sound like?

I am the page
Poems are tattooed across my body
I am the finished sentence, the thought
Entire to itself.

In me, there is your past;
In me, your future.
I am light, deflected off the page
Which fulfills you with its blankness

The Unfinished

The light divides us
From such airs
As midnight clings to.

You can only write what you love.
I'm not saying   it isn't
Hard.
But you can only write what you love.

In this picture is a man taking
Breath, a woman leaning.

I sing this out of tune.
It is alluvial & wrenching.
I sing this out of breath.
Its measure will come later.

That crook of the tree over
There
Does not interest me. Would it
Interest you?

Better these rocks
Under it, sporting
Dull colors— like men's clothing.

What good are these

Unfinished gestures— the decay of

Objects & buildings?

They are contained

By us, in riven

Earth. Where night divides

From what light clings to.

Do we inhabit buildings

Or do they inhabit us?

Hearing the sound

Of no one's

Voice— breath that it

Contains.

What I regret does not encompass horns. We are here, inside an emotion, as a fly is frozen in deep amber. At the apparent book with no sound crushing. As a brick is crushed methodically, cruelly by a child. We experience waves. We are not singing. We are singing to an absence, a black void in the heart of the Metroplex. The Metroplex is endless & uncrushable. It has replaced cities because we cannot dream outside its outlines, its silly edges, its decayed, bright plastic.

No one is real. Can I remain broken in this dysphoria? Then whom shall I speak to, to remain open?

I did not know the 'you' to whom I had addressed these outcomes. She appeared so suddenly— like a ghost of my future. The violent waves angularly strike the point at which our memories seem aimless & uncrushable. To look for the point of a greater launching. To build this, although outside of time, for an instant, in the flesh-book which has been torn open. Which seizes distant memories trapped at the roots of mad wallpaper. Which causes clouds to interact with a child's haywire imaginings.

Once we are here, you don't expect an easy resolution. & In fact, none ever is— the ghosts just want you to think that: to give up, go on with your business, to keep moving at all costs, but toward no point in particular. The cries of strangers are never so real as those of friends & celebrities, anyway. Then to give up now, in the uncanceled passage? Where the Metroplex stays open after dark— stays incessantly open. We are the People so where we are is populated with us. We remember what makes sense, & just so much. We are reproductions of the reproductions of ourselves (becoming populated). Don't go out there. It never was.

This continuous dissolve, in your slipping along in the air where no one jitters. We were meant to depart? Where there is no here, only desert & the outside. The outside is caused by money; you can buy it, & then it will be the inside. You can annex or invade, to make it inside what you already know. So the outside is always & only pregnant with its own interior. It is the removable barrier which we'll come to pretend was always & naturally not there.

Daylight is for the collection of objects. This is important because such activity makes days pass quickly.

We are visible to ourselves & others, though not seen. We are displayed cautiously, at angles the perceiver already knows.

Night is the absence of such activity— or what we least suspect.

The sun goes down to encourage waking. Those things which can't be pictured.

The Unfinished

To sing to ourselves while the dead inform us
Although we are not here
Although we sing, at a transitive distance
While we are naked, being dreamed.

By whom? Our guardian imposters?
By the weight of cities which can't bear us?
When you go to sleep, do you sleep?
Being awake, though artless in the postures

Of unthinking selves' positions
We don't take. If we do take anything,
It would have to be something there's
No word for.

Describe. Defile. Deny. I can't
Do any of these
Things seriously,
Until the weather changes character—

Our positions in the archives rendered
Useless by material
Flinging. If there is a *we;*
If there is a *place.*

I'm afraid of numbers & bumblebees,
Of tightly resolved cities,
Of the impositions of selves on others
Spread

Wide like daydreams of the obscene
Parade, "that old-time religion,"
Or anything else we wish we'd
Said.

Patenting objects for reply
Until the weather changes character.
To refuse
Abandoned futures, root them

In the ground.

BOOK V.

For what's not gathered

The Unfinished

To continue, if it continues, into
Traffic being finished
At the construction.

When we talk, we talk of old men
Relinquished futures
Whirlwinds

Desert polyglots
Restaurant lounge amours
& All that pleasure would suggest

Where the flesh of writing stirs
The memory, the tongue

A rapture which the page accepts
Although it is now still-born
Seeking finer intuitions

The world goes on outside us
Then we go on
Until it is song

The Unfinished

The marvel at the side of a reference

Is all used up. We can disown its voice,

Its unkempt gardens. No one tells you to

Stop channeling the past,

You just decide to do it one day,

& It works. If you ride that

Particular train, a fly will enter

The car window & leave

By the opposite door. Does that

Smear of ink on your finger

Mark you

As an un-twentyfirst century

Poet? Rain today

Or grimy. The hand waves.

It is announcing its condition, by writing.

It is nothing more than a name,

A device that smells of musk.

Terrible. Wedged into summer.

Listen to the rains which strike. This is

No accident. For some

Who have considered leaving,

Now would be the time. It occurs

Frequently, & nothing pulls

It out of character. You

Cannot teach it; you cannot

Touch it; yet it is always

You.

The Unfinished

I cast a spell: *Tonight*
Snow will not fall;

We could awaken
In grave delight—

But snow will not fall
Tonight.

•

Then how is future glimpsed
With all of history driving past?

To cast
Reflections from such swaying

Pomegranate trees
While also standing

Beside
The future of unloveliness—

•

These days whose names are still not spoken

Such as yours, my future

Preserver, my previous

Dark lake or fraying—

The Unfinished

There is a crack in my windshield
        Which reflects
Light differently than
        Windshield proper.

This occurs despite the names
        Of several
                Flora I don't know

•

To be nothing without light, but keep revolving
Under the silence of bees
In spaces before ghosts are formed—
Ghosts composed of daylight.

•

The shrill varieties of names;
Inflected surfaces of brick—
A chiaroscuro pattern,
Daylit

& The company of bees
In flowers' tuneless variety
Of an afternoon—
& The color under the trees.

The Unfinished

To have immediately all been here

In destinies of ghost-light

Before singing— an elegantly corruptible landscape

Against which questions verge

The work is pieced together from dust

It converges with the earth

It does not name the corpses of the cities driving past

It lacks all good intention

To be doing everything all at once

Is an intervention against speech

Rebellion without suffering

Where we aren't sung

The Unfinished

Make a list of the things of this world.*

Imagine yourself among them, touching

Them, smooth or coarse— leaving

Ink upon your fingers.

Remember other afternoons

You fought; remember

The succession of afternoons,

---

* chicory
 bubblegum wrappers
 trading cards
 soot
 a birthday cake
 frost on car windshield at morning
 breakfast cereal w/ extra sugar
 lamppost
 helium
 permanent markers & their permanent markings
 branches fallen from trees after storm
 daisies (old-fashioned)
 antique car mysteriously parked on street
 valium
 ocean liners
 whiff of cumulous, at sky's edge
 basket, hung from tree perhaps
        as bird feeder (there are no birds)
 dime on car floor
 empty, nonrecyclable bottle
 mirror, needing to be cleaned
 sheets of construction paper, never used
 computer, outdated, in junk heap
 garage door opener (needs batteries)
 butterscotch
 a child's sailboat

Each unique & interchangeable,
Until the ghosts arrive.

They connect objects with their pasts— misshapen
In particular ways, which strangely

Carry the taste of fennel,
The smell of some unspeakable perfume

Shut for years in a musty room.
We imagine a narrative which connects

These facts
Somehow— the room was owned by a frail

Old woman who died—
But the truth is it won't work.

Junk is junk. What smells
Festers & grows worse. It doesn't

Matter if we
Understand. It doesn't

Matter if objects
Understand us. We live

With forgeries to invent ghosts

Who make peace with our dead.

To still be held, against an atrocity. Some of this is vague. Things go on without repeating. *One atrocity leads to another, I know.* Some of this is whispered. In childhood, it was simpler— this folly, the seemingly ambient skies. At the edges of some moment we aren't sure. This is a lyrical fable.

This is a fable, but not lyrical. It's been reported from the front that you don't breathe. One of our poets is here to investigate, though his grasp of the material is not certain. The material is uncertain. It's formed by skies which are fleeting. It is formed by oceans, gulls or pieces of brick affixed to great white sheets of paper. Nightfall is a coincidence of sleep— a tenuous redaction to the unspoken notions already at stake. The moon does not trust us [yet]. The sun is yellow. The atrocities are hidden behind a curtain ~~camera~~. To hear them whimpering ~~to form a public language~~ we have to keep them there.

This is a private language. Death is speaking. There is oil to burn. This is silent, so it forms a rupture. Its alternative is silence, but not rapture. On the condition of speaking publicly without saying anything. The alternative will not ~~yet~~ drown ~~us~~. It is a public sentencing. Burning, as in silence. *To dream where shadows forge the edges of the rain.* Burning, as in life [faces you don't come back to]. No one sees all the dead faces, the dead gulls who don't cry. Yet we lie awake in silence. Waiting for history to erupt.

The Unfinished

What you write on is your choice

What you write improves your vision

Except where clouds mark us

Like passages of dream

In the attractions of things which

Wouldn't be standing

Except where cities fail us,

Move together & pry open

What you write on, palpably, is coincidence

In the repetition of dreams not viable

Although we choose irruptive features

Which leave us in the dark

What you write fucks with your ambition

Until the dead give way

& Are held inside our voices;

Then we become landscapes of fire & salt

When you write, if you are dead, sign here

To notify the arrivals

The still mortified transcriptionists

Who claim your speech as their own

When you write, your speech is dead on arrival

Reconstituted but iffy

As if all the salt fell off your flesh

To give you back your tongue

The Unfinished

Find the verb that defaces night

Place it on your tongue

Like a host

Like a ghost— to draw your breath in quiet

Hunger from the sentence

The sentence is merely an appendage

It haunts you under midnight without charm

It dissolves sleep, but cannot wake you

From what still devours breath

Ghosts devour what you only can surrender—

An unspoken record at which we shatter

To swallow our own tongues (in private)

Until only earth forgives, or can keep still

The Unfinished

The night increases what it does not own

It desires the lack

It lacks while still increasing what we burn

It does not get enough

It drones on while reading its own poems

It is barbaric factures without grace

It wears too much perfume

It jounces when it should not speak

It whistles when you do not fear it

It thinks you should; it cajoles then startles you

It wants to be the president some day

It wants you to understand how much this means

It is good

It is good for you

It is so good of you to come. The night

Is not what it pictures or consumes

Except mostly when the air is quiet

& It's there again, at the window, waiting—

The Unfinished

If I try to tell you everything,
Am I being honest with myself?

Moon interspersed with body:
Picture it.

We demand everything from our poems,
Then demand our poets be silent.

Distance agitates the light,
A sort of bleakness, when looked at the right

Way. The right light. What
Light is right to now disrobe

Our future selves, stealth lovers, skies
Of intricate elision?

Sensation drives us to breathe—
No yesterdays, no destinations,

Silence or
Release.

The Unfinished

There are no more of us here.
  The cities have been ghosted
    We breathe, in quick
      Succession. Faces
        Appear, but are not needed.
          Even the dead give way, though they have
            Other occupations.

There are no more of us here—
  In erratic laughter driven
    By daylight's vast
      Deplorable sideshow
        When we populate the night
          With these
            Faces or distractions.

  No one
    Is useful to himself who
      Can go on this way.

The Unfinished

There are still no more of us
Being here, though we are transfixed
In dead summer's lapsing
In gray weather up to the eaves.

Being here, one isn't serious.
It is a complex interchange— this being
& Singing, & being one with the animals
& All this going forth.

I'll say it again: who are you, part
Sea urchin, part ghost of the violated
Quarters of cities
You have yet to dwell in?

Speak to me vigorously, as if you had only a minute
To say anything paramount.
I'll excuse myself 'til I can't breathe;
I'll create a place where the accounts can be dropped off.

When you get the call
You don't have to listen—
Only now & then sigh, as if
Pretending to understand.

The Unfinished

This relentless vanishing
At cities' margins,
At the borders of a page.

The paper will not
Take the ink.
It is pining for a means

To channel this erasure,
A discomfit at which we're nearly sure
Who 'we' is, but not much

Else, besides this sucking
Sound going on which we'll call
A temporary departure,

The draft of the draft of a breakdown.
To ease against our temporal remains
& Dislocations of same—

Of 'city,' 'margin,' 'nightfall.'
Each unto each, permitting time
(Which unfortunately we don't have).

We disappear, into the margins or edges of the name we bear. We hear, but cannot describe. We seem to be in great, lacquered boxes until the night goes out.

(Night is a character in this poem, although it's in prose.)

Can we bear this night, or its field of description? I am calling out your name. The sun is ready to dream this. We are a dream of the sun. We are born with various delusions which it is the business of night to rectify.

Rain has started to trace the outlines of the buildings.

Night is no excuse to not come back.

To bear the positions of the wind which frees us.

Which seizes us. Twists out the root of this language.

This language only spoken by the dead.

The Unfinished

To insist on more than can be said—
The bulk of light at the outlines of the tongue,
The way the wind encases buildings
At the edge of silence & release

At the séance edge, where ghosts become spectators
& We gnaw black windows to invent seeing
'Til what we see becomes excess
& The borders of the tongue are crashed

############################

This *more*, voracious & uncrushable
It wounds you in the lips of night like flinging
It seethes against the contours of a violence
It waits for you amid dark flowers

Dark voices at the edges of what's stopping you
Until the architecture flattens all perspective
& Fulfills you with its hunger,
Its voracious lust, its insatiable *MORE*—

The Unfinished

To spill the flower & the echo

To drive in silence while engines bleed

To divorce singing from the weight of the vulva

To become engorged with humid decibels

Where night devours, & we become

The agents of our ineluctable hauntedness

Gone blind in cities of mad perspective

Filled, then swallowed with the hunger of bees

Until shadow's agency defaces need

& We become pregnant with a thousand cities

While still molesting clocks & hummingbirds

Who echo blindness in mad reply

after Vallejo

The Unfinished

I'm finished. You

  Are a means of taking

   Breath.

       Hunger

     Is drawn from the matter. It is a necessary

      Condition. Clouds which fit

       Like jigsaw pieces, into

        The manes of the trees.

It changes, in the way skies look

  At you. When they look at you,

   Skies are

    Most serious. Destinations

     Of the trees call back

      To you. You saunter, & fall forward.

       It is necessary to provoke, then startle, you.

In this way, the Poem's work gets done.

The Unfinished

The mirror gets my light

It spoils the image with its dark reversal

It sleeps instead of me

It burns the reflections of dead men laughing

Dead men do not often laugh

Mirrors frighten them to sleep

We look up at them with faces of ash

We can hear the fire breathing

To stand, reflected but never there

To be burned by the nape of the moon without drowning

In pools where color suddenly spills

Out, & a dark hand grasps at stars

The Unfinished

Dark like the ripple

Where the moon flies off

Dark like memory—

Ghosts in blond summer

Dark like the reflections of what

Stirs you

Dark in light, in afterlight—

This residue which absence leaves behind.

The Unfinished

I want to think black & white in old movies,

In the graceful cries of birds.

I want the wind to kiss my jacket.

I want to know I am not dreaming

When I am not. I want

The weather to encompass horns.

I want the moon's sensation not to burn

My tongue. I want noon to learn

The moves of dancers on an August night.

I want to think in great strips of color,

In accidents of neon.

I want poetry to scald my lungs.

I want midnight to be critical. I want

To study the ancient

Parlances of bees. I want to burn all

Hesitation in gallons of moonlight.

I want to sleep until the ocean

Drowns in wakefulness,

Until I reinvent myself laughing

In daylight upheld by critical Januaries

Born upon the tongue.

The Unfinished

Borne upon the page
The reactions of falling shapes
Their orbital hunger, which casts
No reflection
Their silent village
Marked by tongues

To be embedded in the night
In absent cities which imagine us
Which people us
In dark necessity
Until we flee into what hunger
Imagining a place that's void of light

To hunt within its shadows
To study the infractions of winter
Where vending is still possible
To invent a place of negative summer
Peopled with distractions
Cold distances which draw our very breath

Breath, which follows us
Breath, which cannot be pictured
Open it & scream
When you lose it you will know the answer
At the place where our tongues meet
& Nothing ever is pictured

²³So what? Or whom? & To what end? The ends which come of raw beginnings. Poetry is a ledge. Jump quickly. Being on the spot, or spotted. What end does it describe? Or does it end, & why? It is coming from the source, & not that pure. Everything becomes writing— that table, perhaps, or the door. I had thought what?— but now it's not. Now it's knotted, like estuaries. Like vestiges which pry the rains apart. The rain is not a part of this poem. Wind falls down. To think in streams of summers rushing. To use summer as a material. A dead heat, swallowing the eaves. Under the placemats of what grieves. To grieve for all of time passing, or to burn like summer, swift & indelicate. To feel the crashing of words upon the tongue. Never to be won.

²⁴What are cities made of words? Whom did you call? What love frees us— being freed or fleeing in the attractions without charge? Without mechanics, without voice. Our cities fail us, as do our journals full of ghosts. Light falls on the roof slates blithely. It is indifferent to its role in poetry. (This was not always the case.) We are charged with the creation of animal cities. Our cities, like our selves, are often stolen. Stolen, at the intensity of looking at light for the first time ever. A red toenail; a subjective barrage.

The Unfinished

It rains a little in the repugnant mirror

Where hemispheres want no reflection

But enter a world so it appears

Reflected to them as an eclipse on paper—

The only way to see it which

Does not burn your eyes

Your gaze is part of this distraction

Be it carbon or animal

A chair was put there by the door

So we can trip over it

The moon landing was predicted

In our imaginations of the earth in orbit—

Summer a mirage in rain's

Condensation on car windows. To kindle in our hearts

The pages are soggy with memory

With the attributions of the trees

& A need to burn what's irreplaceable—

Sodden furniture, dry twig's breath.

To fill the night with old distractions;

Changing faces of the moon.

The Unfinished

In which we don't see, until it was there

At last— or entering the descriptive environment

As a shadow-form etched down the blinds

At midafternoon precisely   what we see

When we see it, is materially the question

Lunar & insurgent, the break   in the flow of the matter

It resulted in; & then   then somewhat mirrored

Back on the flesh, which was formed   from the upload. From upheaval.

It hadn't been the first time.   Maybe nobody watched it

Set it in place with the pinwheels & smoke detectors.

Maybe it had never really been there. Or—

Materialized is a strong word— taken place at least

In the form you'd suspect   you'd be able to see, else conduct

Photomagnetic energy to a point   lips touched   & we'd see

     The eclipse from a break in the retinal   wall

Where what sounds is freely given   in the streets—

          A distribution of new mirrors

At which light cannot be won.

²⁵It was never merely to have chosen. In the constraints without singing. Where daylight is a musical instrument, a mutable chromatic whisper, a breach of solitude. Solitude, as something to be fled or attained? I worry about you, & can admit this finally to the sound of wind in the pine needles. A sound almost like waves crashing (there are no waves, only proscriptive nostalgias). The light turns itself off, & everyone has fled. Then you arrive, before there is a 'there' to be sung to.

²⁶I'm not sure the useful parts of noise add up. I mean that you or I cannot add them. I mean that you too are impermanent. I mean that dusk settles all around us. It settles; we are settled. What's consumed settles quickly. In the intonations of this light or afterthought. *For 'light,' insert 'night.'* For 'settled,' read a civilizing gesture. To still be settled, in the dusk which fits precisely. Against our still impassive fingertips. Less fidgety than micromanagement. Than braille, which is forgotten. Than shudders we've been forged against. Erased, as all impermanent villages. Civilizing, conquered.

²⁷I forgot I was writing the poems that I love. I need to sleep— but not just yet. Does hunger cause redemption or incision? What final emergency stops this train? I seem to prefer questions to disquisition. ~~To disintegration?~~ Quiet as butterflies' knees— the tone in which I speak mimics popular symmetry, which I don't proffer.

²⁸What I prefer is wrapped in the surfaces of a rhythm without gain. It is a songbook or a careless thread. Ghosts are entering paranormal workdays with memories stuck between their teeth. Do you hear them, even now, creating the fear of outside silence? ~~For 'silence,' misread 'science.'~~ In linked gestures which are silent as the fear of bees. What stutters, or [still] dies laughing. Under words' stunted forms?—

The Unfinished

The work shall be indelicate or not at all
An art of swallowing the moon

It appears here on your face
Aligning with all sexy happenstance

Where we want what we want, but cannot swallow
Counted happenings, the feints

At which our trousers become aware
Like smoke across all futures

Against now impassible cities
A subterfuge effacing night's

Dark organs without reeling
Upon the erased bird cliffs all screaming is natural

Being refugees now disguised as salt
It appears here on your face

Although we sometimes are unaware
As if you or I were chalk birds

All reified selves lacking smoke
In the locus of what swirls

The Unfinished

Earth, that's dredged up from this night;
Night, with its 10,000 arrivals—

Like interstices which leave
Us blank—
Blank like dry tin,
Like neon rotors no one notices.

We are in charge of this now, the unfinishing
Trees which drive us mad,
Tender or awake
In the subjunctive nature of the bees

Who dance, being forthright
In the interstices which slip
Between
Like blanks which skip while no one breathes.

The Unfinished

As if to merge, by chromatic difficulties

Wherever salt is inflicted

In order to put off a new beginning

A nude being, a driven economy

Emptied, at the edges of what's seen

At a sated delivery. To deform the picture

Requires a particular violence. These

Ink smears. The heart beating steadily.

Whenever I say *they*, I include also

Possibilities of dust,

A need to deform articulation

Out of the air which draws

Us blank—

Pale as all hunger

Of words no one whispers,

Even to the dead.

————

My zero sum game has blasphemed the reflection.

I glance, in euphony

At the unsteady parade.

Households are naked. I can't take

Much more of it.

———————

Come here, mouth— you black hole gaping;

Come here, all holes of any

Kind.

I will taste you, one by one

I will deform, & be deformed

In the hunger of new worlds

———————

An occult & orderly distraction

Where the green worlds rang—

I am a child of this distinction

I am an ox, born in summer;

I am an impalpable district, your body's

Residue

Which I leave, to speak in private

To the unlikely cactus

Flower

Thrust into summer's remains.—

BOOK VI.

For restless foresight

The Unfinished

In the distance between poems
Silence speaks.
It stitches a new tongue for you;
It wants memory to be private.

It wants. But I cannot afford
It. Its mouth is shaped like rain.
It wants to know the interior of a terror
      Of not speaking;
It wants to give what it does not return—

A ruined *it*. Listen to it; listen
To its hunger.
Listen to want driven private.
Listen to the voice above

The language of the bees.
Listen, the dull ache.
Listen to what I don't regret.
Listen to the ruined bones

Inside its skull which vibrate
When you hear the name
Of what you do not own—
The distance, unnamed, of what you know
      You need.

The Unfinished

The horizon does not make. It
Is always singular.
It extends where we do not yet mean
To go. But we do
Go, & are
Bent up. It's April Fool's Day
Or it will be, if we wait
Long enough. How long is
Enough? What time
To sing, or say how much we flee
Amid flowers & pillars & salt
With dusk catching in the
Throat? If we wait, the boat
Will sail, & we'll be free
Of this horizon—
Like ghosts in cities
Yet to be made, occult
Faces of clocks.

The Unfinished

What's unfinished lives at the point of departure.

It creates absence, a fiercely unmet need.

It is a city of buildings, each having only three sides

Where night is composed of what you want. You want

It composed in fragments of a departure

In the trees. This song it sings:

> *When the trees go away,*
>
> *When there's no thing left but the heat of the day,*
>
> *When the oceans are our monuments*
>
> *& Our monuments are dumb as salt,*
>
> *Then shall it be finished,*
>
> *& We'll be filled with glacial silence—*
>
> *The discharges of our heat upon knowing*
>
> *& The dead, singing nothing—*

÷

The dead, in fact, do not sing

Except just around your bedframe.

They claim to be Iraqi civilians

But you want to see their passports,

To feel beneath their tongues, lest some

Explosive

Be hidden there.

÷

Be hidden there, my salt-lover,
My ghost-lover, my non-Iraqi visitor

Banish me till sunrise
When even ghosts weep

The Unfinished

Time flees, in a parallel motion

To its source. The days are hidden

From the night. Earth reaches round the

Sun, but never reaches what it seeks

~~Never seeks what it will~~

~~Need~~. But still we go round

& Round— stopped, in a parallel

Commotion— an occult ruin, really

Where the eyes of passengers are captured

Before the moment of escape.

When we escape, we are still inside

The condition of our passing. Night

Creates more desires than it

Buries. Light consumes you, buried

In its passing

Vivacity. What you do not create

Devours you. There is no more *I* or *we*;

There is *you*, hidden, laughing.

& When you wake you break

All the notices,

The conditions of all breath upon the tongue;

& When you dream, you're a participant

In a failed, romantic notion

Which, though 'romantic,'

Is real. Afraid of summer

In the ghost-light, with dim

Shoppers drifting

Past—

The Unfinished

Completion strangles the need to go

Past; it arranges Us

Inside him

        Them/ or are

    At the point we

Is, or becomes [one] strangled ~~startled~~.

If one is strangled, or even somewhat estranged

One cannot CONSUME

        Cannot, not, cannot contain

Contained. Be entertained—

❖

[To arrange him in its noise of trapped flowers]

❖

[It's the noise which must, somehow, be crossed out]

❖

Art is at a standstill.

It cannot devise speech.

It's still beholden to what

    Settles;

It wants to find a way to mess things up—

But it cannot

Get out of its

Art habits. It thinks that writing

Less is writing more

Concisely. It wants what it

Wants, until it

Changes;

It has developed quite a habit

Of care without caring;

It is thinking of becoming a snake, or smoke.

Let us all think of becoming

Smoke. Or ash. Or smoke becoming

A rendez-vous/residue.

But what's left is next to you

Bent by air until it exchanges

Spends. Spreads interplay. The—

The interrupt outside of what

Hungry pale encounter?

The Unfinished

I.

What slips is   spoken residue

At an edge or loss for

           Almost-becoming

An almost-loss: city with unnamed edges

City exiting at the crossouts

     Which labor under my tongue

City igneous with breath or hair

At this dream-city I'll world you— ghost broken vowels

I'll erase light 'til it becomes habit   wrapped

In neon

     I'll leave a border at the vicinity of

Spaces uninhabited

       I'll become wraith to your demon

& Bring you

     A bundle of words— worlds blooming wildly

When your eyes are smoke

When there is no 'here' which can exhibit 'now'

When we've invented new names for *moon* & *rope*

       Then our city shall be real

& Burn mad in noon's eye

II.

Imbricate weave in the lake.

Lake, glaring

      In thought

Alight with winter, which is almost animal

         So pure is it,

So barren of design.

          A lake becomes our city

At the vicinity of touch & blur

      A barren motion of perhaps space

Bleeding through the other side

Of the page

        The page is perhaps a land.

        Our land. your land. my land.

But land, in any   event you fell in

You fell in over & over.

      A city needs some land

Fallen, into the sand.

III.

But what is trapped, down underneath our city—

City born in light?

      The name of tomorrow

      Is never sure.

I'll wrap it, I'll enter

It in thought-marrow.

I'll announce its breakdown, for all

       Who hold the door & look.—

What is trapped, in dizzy dark folds

Becoming air or speech—

Speech, an almost recess-stillness—

            Mockery of umber

Bleeding shadows from its ink.

     Transformed in bodies' dark becoming

Toward our city, violent blur—

The Unfinished

This business of intractable humming,

Lying like a jaguar in the sun.

The jaguar doesn't blink. He still

Awaits astonishment,

Expects it; yet he moves

                In states

Of predatory grace.

He identifies with the hunted— slower

Creatures who succumb

      For his hunger, his desire, his

Need ever burning.

      •

The jaguar speaks

Portuguese & Greek,

& His native, jaguar tongue.

The jaguar is not easily

      Amused. He moves

Slowly, when the purpose strikes;

He conserves speed & wantonness,

Yet he *is* desire—

        Stealth sunlit blanketed.

The Unfinished

What still grapples, in the language of

               Trapped things—

To be so radiantly present

          Yet trapped, in space which

Touch implodes

               But trapped, in emblematic space

         A place implied by jaguar light

A silver warmth—

              Place, with nerves lit

Place of hard leisure, hurried trysts

         Of summer's absence stinging

Place of hornets shrouded in   gratuitous debris

             Until light becomes you. Until you become

                  The sacrifice

What have I sacrificed

             For the poem, lately? What

        Have you? What sacrifice

                  Is artifice

Underwritten by silence? To have been preoccupied

        By different currencies.

To draw in or refuse

             This silence. All these measures

All these ways to blast & burn

        The tongue from (vague)

             Earth, unwritten.—

The Unfinished

It's time for more. Yet hunger's at
A standstill. If you wake
You wake to still more striking. Everything
Is overture

Or normative— a failed transition
Bitten off the tongue
Of words, words which fail us
Even as we no longer reply.

~

To flee is life— though we mistake
The linnets for the gumshoes,
Artifice for the refusal
To sit still.

When we sit still we're doing what
We're told;
Sit still mentally, we leave a lack
For the entertainment to fill.

The way to be filled by entertainment
Is to think, lackingly.
The lack can take up all your time. It is an
Acquiescence

A permission not to wonder. It filters

What's predetermined

For you. The expect.—

Letting you sleep when still awake

But fingering what-have-you

In passive resolution—

Image

Of crisis on a screen.

The Unfinished

When I finish this I will be normative

When I finish, slender threads will be broken

When I'm finished, I'll spy into the heart of the needle

When I finish, silence which is redundant

When I finish, will there be a sense of loss

                 in the windows of passing trains?

When I finish this I won't repeat myself, standing on wires

When I finish, will it finish me?

When I finish this, a part of it willingly?

When I finish this, apart from the conditions of its inception

When I finish, ragged eyes of strangers *as if there are strangers*

When I finish, ambergris winter afternoon

When I finish, different from where I became

When I finish, made to stutter or inflect

When I finish this, in the passage of slow days

When I finish, incrementally

When I finish, vivid in hindsight

When I finish this, in fragile blocks of summer

When I finish this, until I am not born

When I finish, in harmonic distraction

When I finish, let the wind speak

The Unfinished

The plot of this world must   go on, must

    Go on, into plotless air

In plotless air we imagine   ~~ingeminate~~   blown apart largely

       In impositions of breath   who explode

The plot the part of it   incident to go

   & Go on repeatedly   & incident to go

& Still go on, & outward toward a subject, & the air apart

     From it   the air, & subject   implacable, bent

       Up in its sight   pushed apart

     In the air that's teeming & repeated

          Bitten, in order to repeat that part

      & So implode, in glints of clouds

Over air   seemingly on paper

            & The onrushing

    Silence, the sluice.   the slew.

The slew inside its plot itself   is magenta   night is silence

    The repeat penetrable as tattered buildings

Is a start toward its plot its parted   happenings

        Glint over surfaces of earth on paper

    To implode   in its general reflection   what changes over time

Changes tractable as repeating

     Earth as night repeating

There were tangible parts of the not-finished— cities broken or recomposed. Our sense of place changes with the way we have changed it. It, this where, is what to us— in the future, in our past? What past is future ~~furtive~~? Erosion, landfills & construction. What structures are furtive (strict, tentative)? What space now weighs us to the ground?

The stanzas imagine a place that holds us there; cities hold us. Do they imagine us? Are we imaginable? We are a different species than the cities, our monster-creatures. We are not the Metroplex, though it resembles
                    Us (we being its fathers, its mothers—

        As someone breathes, & can remember

A time before the tract homes ~~built us~~

                We being the tractable

The birthed, unbent to constraints
                                        Of place

            Unmarked by human need.

The Unfinished

People ask me to name what

    Means

Who go on in luminous night

      Who go

People pass, like dawns into winter

In the pass   /the passage   go

Clearer   mistaken like its every form

     Ghostlier   as thought must echo

         Or scratch out

Unlike what, restlessly, isn't here

       Torn apart, at the wings

(The wings: incessantly mythological forms

Torn a part   ~~at art, into echo~~

    The intake where we are rushing

To go

           Go blindly into salt

     ~

When we go—

    When we are blind, emboldened

  Then disappear into salt

When we have inherited currencies of love & light

     When breath itself has vanished

     When we have escaped, into driftless air

     When past is no more, & no more the present

     When houses are made of salt, & our lungs break

Only then shall we see salt or flesh as air;

Only then shall we sing in color, into summer's darkest wounds

The Unfinished

Yet she is finished, suddenly—

Let it go   let it go on, into light

Let night merge into   all of us

Let light in here   *let the night have her*

     & Smoke   let smoke curl round her head

Illumined   her 'here' & ghosted

      Radiance, her smoke   body her ash

Body here in the first   the place, the lit

Inside *let it night her*   & ash

      & Flesh, to ash, & her

   Face   radiant round & living

I refuse to understand this   *isn't*

Refuse   to understand her   *not-here*

   Refuse all useless time

     & Being   I remember her here, & being

Laughing   remember her here & singing

     Why here?   Why poems (her sudden form of grace?

The poems from her breath which are still here

       Not her   *why?*

It's that *why* that stops me cold

   Is what keeps stopping   ~~stop me~~   ~~grieving~~

Let her, the night, in here

Let her in, that she is gone

Let her go now, that she has won

      & It is sung, & will be

Let it go now, that she is   *was*

Let night have her, her body done—

        She will go on,

                But let her

                         Akilah Oliver (1961-2011)

To understand through incompletion, the partial harboring of a list or name. To make the list be frightened of the poem. To make of the poem a circuit for the perception of fleeing matter. Of energies depleting.

For 'name' insert to make increasingly real. The real increases what's not burned. For instance, insert the fact that you are not burning, dear reader, or at least I hope.

Whenever you think something is inescapable, exhaust all possibilities.

The moon has not been named thus far. I would place it on my tongue.

Write a composition on the forms that silence takes. Become immersed in noise. Bleed only when the need describes a city. The city is a complex exchange. It is a host, entirely resistant to architecture. It is a means of going forward, a clap of wayward grace, an intent to occupy (or become occupied). If you become occupied, think hard about the needs of the occupiers. If you become lost, enter a city so that you will know where you are, what limits you reside in. The bleeding limits, going forward into silence made of words. The wind, in the reversal of complex trees.

The Unfinished

The ghost-buildings are still here
We don't know a way to address them
They stare at us yes really stare
They will never go away

To go away, at the onset of speech
To stare with ghost-window-eyes
To be truly naked in the telling
Or speak, at the onset of being dreamed

If you dream. If you speak. If you
Enter ghost-space (language is a ghost)
The space of the story that you weave
To enter or depart

Depart in hunger of words apparitionally
In economies of *having been seen*
Depart in violent day-rhythm lurking
While mislaying the proportions of the shadows of the bees

The Unfinished

To sing by what comes crashing

In the room without going away

The room is full of forms

It is like my body (my body contains

Likenesses) & it

Is somewhere else

Broken like the terrain

The broken or contiguous night

With stars all flowing past

The past is real like summer

& The taverns are full of light

To help construct this space

& Be gone, in a noise or motion (final

Light or line we keep erasing—

The Unfinished

This noir light that bathes us

That evenings us in daylight

Sky of glass

Windmill light, bracing us

In desolate, impassive care

How live it up, in untidy

Cloud window form

While the day repeats the obvious

Restlessly, in air

The Unfinished

Becoming the visible

> Gift

When you wake accordingly

Conclusive as the light   you wear it

> Light, you wear it

> Filmy

& Gradual, in its pre-solstice arrangements

Night inserts itself into this

> Codex

The imagination reigns us in

To be conclusive is not to imagine   to

> Construct   to wear in light

To wear the light as a symbol   one must say

One must say silvery stars

> Slivered selves

One must weigh the sounds as one says

> This slivered

> Silver silvery stars arrayed

This codex at which we are) by night (inserted.

The Unfinished

When you go to sleep   *when you*

      Deep in blush

  Of air   *go thou*

When you go, or do admit

          This ghost

  Who is no more

    But is bound in   to this codex, at the start

     When you end, or admit cruelly

Time's passage, that binds us

        That you are bound, here

      To these things which emit

Light   light at the end

       Of the thread, the face

           This

Passage into sleep

     When you do   go there

When you go, with birds on your face

When you go, or do admit

      This leaving & being in time

When you go, in passage to this space

    This place, this edge where we don't dream

  But when you do, go now—

The Unfinished

The scar is what we imagine it

To be. The light goes scarcely

Through wind. When you sear

Or scare, you can disappear

Into wind in a parallel

Motion to its

Trace. The plan is to seed

In bloom of thought

Embedded. That's not true; you *are*

Embodied, &

The thought *is* you. Appear then

In necessities of sight, &

Move as love, into darkening light.

The Unfinished

The darkness of the world is stoppered

To feed on ghosts in the afternoon light

Before going away. When you go, fall down.

When you fall down, sing

To be dreadful. I question the fault

Between civics &

Migration.

If you hear the dead, speak back, & take note

Of new forms, words

Which no longer stir.

When the words exit, follow them out

From the body. Leave scratchings

So you will know how to get back.

Hide in the shimmer of moist

Bodies, so birds will know

How to disappear.

Wear paint for one day. Let

The dead peel it off.

The Unfinished

The poem is another way of vanishing.
Ghosts do not remember this
Who live
At dark borders of the door.

There is a clock at the edge of the
Bookface. Is it
You
Who's being stopped?

When you are stopped, you are free to begin
Like the poem & its ongoingness. What
Is there   to believe in what
Is there   to stop, or look back at

In your ongoingness the wind does not
Believe you
It sings in the crevices
Of what's explicitly not   when you are

There, you are free to begin
You in air, & books don't wake
      You. The only books that do
Are those not written ~~stillborn~~

When they are written, they line up

& Sing like ghosts

They make city noises out of poems

Which build like rooms when the ghosts wake

The Unfinished

In the room which is unsettlingly divided

(The room is part of a city)

There are locks, & means of going forward

There are chairs, in the event there are some people

In the room who would like

To sit down. Do you want to

Sit down— or I mean, would you

If you were in the room?   The room

Is a balance of extremes

Being part of the city. It is

There all the time, & *of* you, & you are

There, & slowly becoming an occupant,

Tender & sharp, inside the room's divisions,

Its antiseptic grace. The room revolves—

It gathers speed around you.

Room is a form of terror, keeping

What's outside out

What's inside in

Don't go out; it's roomier here

We are alight & singular

Locations within vacancies

To leave but never go (astir)

Darkly into rain

The Unfinished

and one alone will speak of being
born in pain
and he will be the wings of an extraordinary liberty
—Frank O'Hara

To still go on, in states of delivery

Until deliverance informs a structure

Becoming uninformed, or uniform

In the delivering rain

The time that's left is always there

We lag behind, consuming it

In order to spit it out in air

Which frees us from our breath

Your birth, & ours, is omnipresent

Until you reappear

Into sky like bird flocks   in the

Everything that's already here

for Jack Collom at 80

The Unfinished

Is it, in the minutes we don't

Pass, into a space, a city (city

Which is partly imagined)?

Is it, in the moment of its

Parting? Is it that we don't go

When we go? Is it out of tune?

Is it what remains?

Is it capable of being put

Into words? Is it what you thought

You needed, but now don't?

Is it what you needed

To think, until now? Is it what

Remains of night

(Night, which embodies us)?

Is it that the Earth & Sky

Have an empathic relationship?

Is it some kind of residue?

Is it made from what departs?

Is it an act of grace? Is it

Something a child would understand?

Can it be described using words

Like 'glassy' or 'high-strung'?

Is it something you are

Smitten with (someone)?

Is it breakable; & have you broken it

Yet? Does it resemble the moon

On the rim of a shoe?

Is it a stalemate, crossed energies

From which nothing can proceed?

Is it interior to some? Is it frozen?

Do you sometimes wish that it was never there?

The Unfinished

Why can't this be
All of it?

Do the dead have forms of
It (the night

Until we inform them
Of it— we, being venal

Like cities composed of
Partial ruin ~~neon~~

Or cries which strike
Themselves to make

Way for other birds

author photo: Christopher Shugrue

Mark DuCharme was born in Detroit and grew up in its suburbs, the only child of a single mother. He studied with poet/publisher Ken Mikolowski at the University of Michigan, from which he earned a BA, and later at the Jack Kerouac School of Disembodied Poetics at Naropa University, from which he earned an MFA. He is the author of four previous print books of poetry and several chapbooks. Beginning with *The Found Titles Project*, published electronically by Ahadada Books in 2009 but written earlier in that decade, he abandoned the writing of individual and serial poems in favor of what he calls writing projects; *The Unfinished* is his largest writing project to date. His poetry and essays on poetics have appeared widely, and he has been a receipient of the Gertrude Stein Award in Innovative American Poetry and the Neodata Endowment Grant in Literature. DuCharme, who has taught in the Kerouac School's Summer Writing Program, lives, writes, works and teaches along Colorado's Front Range. He has also recently launched a Web site: http://mark-ducharme.com.

Made in the USA
Monee, IL
07 July 2026

56551603R00125